Moving Forward:

From Tragedy to Sunshine

Moving Forward:

From Tragedy to Sunshine

by

Nancy McCarter

Cover Design by Cheryl Perez
Front and Back cover photos by Genna Marie Robustelli
Author photo: Glenda Blackman
Book Design by Cheryl Perez: yourepublished.com

ISBN: 978-1-512-05613-6

First Edition
May 2015

Dedication

This book is dedicated to my daughter, Jacqueline. You have given me the courage and strength to seek out a beautiful future.

Acknowledgments

There are so many people to thank for this book. Thank you to all of my friends who encouraged me and never laughed at my idea to write this book. Thank you Liisa Vexler, my dear friend and published author, who gave me the courage and knowledge to begin this endeavor. Thank you Angela Caravaggio who provided endless support in proofreading and editing. Thank you Genna Robustelli of Tamarindo Family Photos for the amazing cover photo and to good friend and photographer, Glenda Blackman, for the author headshot. And thank you to my wonderful daughter, Jacqueline, who inspires me every day.

Preface

It was 2:30am and I was answering my front door. "Did you find him?" I asked. "Yes" my friend and another guy I didn't know replied. "Is he dead?" I asked. "Yes" they answered.

My boyfriend of 4 years and the father of my young daughter had died. I had 4 hours to process this information before my daughter woke up for her regular day. How is it possible that I find myself in this situation? Where do I go from here?

Chapter 1: Early Years

I was born on December 1st, 1968 in Fort Worth, Texas to young parents who were not expecting to have a child so soon. But here they were, 15 months after having gotten married, assuming the role of mom and dad at ages 21 and 23 respectively.

My mom was from San Antonio, Texas and was born into an upper middle class family in the tony area of San Antonio called Terrell Hills. Her family was pretty social, being members of the San Antonio Country Club with her parents taking frequent trips on cruises and to Europe. My grandparents were lots of fun, cocktails every night at 5, and a well-stocked bar at the house.

My mom was the second oldest of four children. From what I have been told, she lived a good life, had lots of friends, breezed through high school then joined her older sister at a good college in Texas, entering a sorority just like my aunt, her older sister. My mom never got into any trouble. She was a goody two shoes from birth. She never liked to dance or drink, and was always pretty sensible. I came out of the womb ready to party, but more on that later. I definitely take after my grandmother. My mom did have a serious boyfriend all through high school and met and started dating my dad shortly after arriving at college. I had always been somewhat jealous of my mom. It seemed as though she just kind of breezed through life. She quit college after 2 years and got married.

My dad grew up in Shreveport, Louisiana. His family was quite different to my mom's. They were certainly part of the educated middle class, but not nearly as high up on the social ladder. They were much stricter, attending church every week. There was no stocked bar in their house. My dad was the younger of two children. Unlike my mom, he did have an adventurous spirit. I don't know if he drank in high school, but he was a party animal in college. It seems strange to think of him hanging in his fraternity accepting bets as to who could get drunk and be the last one to pass out, when at the same time he was studying to become a protestant minister. But, he had a heart for helping people and I guess that was the avenue he chose at that time. Growing up in the Deep South, he saw firsthand the cruelty of segregation and wanted to do something about it. My mom was blissfully unaware. How the two of them ever came together and fell in love, I still don't understand to this day.

After my parents married, my dad entered seminary and my mom went to work in the secretarial field. The plan was that she would work while he was in school. But, as soon as my mom got accidently pregnant, my dad made her quit working. There was to be no discussion of a working mom, she would stay at home. I have no idea how they lived from a financial perspective, but they did. And from what they tell me, we were all quite happy. We lived in seminary apartments and my mom and I spent our days together doing chores and swimming in the seminary apartment pool, hanging out with other young families. My dad finally graduated from seminary and after a couple of short moves, he landed a permanent job in a little West Texas town called Levelland where he bought a small house. The time we spent here would form my first real memories.

Levelland, Texas was a small town founded in the 1920s. It had a population of 13,000 back in the 1970s which hasn't changed much over the years. Levelland was known for cotton farming and petroleum production. It was a typical small American town, nice hardworking church going people. My dad was the preacher of the First Christian Church of Levelland and my mom stayed home with me.

I was 3 when we moved there. Our small 3 bedroom, 2 bath starter home was in a decent neighborhood and, consistent with the times, I was allowed to explore the neighborhood alone, playing with the other kids. Looking back, it's amazing that we were allowed to do this, but that's just how it was back then. I remember going from house to house playing and riding bikes to somewhat faraway places. It was a typical, idyllic scenario for a young middle class family. My parents were fairly normal. My mom was still a goody two shoes and my dad liked to throw back a couple of beers. We went to church on Sundays and I went to preschool a couple of days a week. When I turned 4 my baby brother was born. I don't remember being happy or sad, but that solidified our family into the perfect mold of Americana.

I went half days to public kindergarten through the week, had lots of friends and was happy. I loved it. My mom took me to school and I rode the bus home. The bus dropped me off about a block away and I walked home from there. I played with friends until dinner or went to tap, ballet, gymnastics, or twirling lessons. Although Levelland was small, it offered everything a 5 year old could want. I loved gymnastics, I loved exploring with friends, and in general I was a happy child. In the summer before first grade, my dad took a job at a larger church in another town. I was crushed. After giving it some thought, my adventurous spirit told me I would be ok and so I welcomed the new adventure.

Brownwood, Texas was founded in the 1850s and when we lived there in the 1970s it had a population of 17,000. It was a 4 hour drive southeast of Levelland. It was still considered West Texas, but being further south, it was warm and green and just big enough to offer a more exciting life for young kids. We had a wonderful backyard full of big trees and a tire swing. I started first grade at South Elementary School and made friends quickly. I was 6 and my brother was 2. I was in Brownies and took piano lessons. I did well in school and really enjoyed life there for 1 ½ years before my dad got another job. This time in another small West Texas town named Hereford.

Hereford was about a 5 hour drive northwest of Brownwood and not too far from Levelland. It is in the Texas Panhandle. Some people mistakenly believe that the Panhandle is the western part of the state that contains El Paso, but it is not. It's the square part at the top of the state bordering Oklahoma and New Mexico. The Texas Panhandle has a culture all of its own. It is dotted with small towns, Amarillo being the center of all things - entertainment, shopping, doctors, you name it. To us, Amarillo was the metropolis, the big fancy city. Hereford was about a 45 minute drive from Amarillo and when you live in the Texas High Plains, a 45 minute drive is nothing. All the small towns in the Panhandle are a part of the same culture. You could meet someone anywhere in the world and if they tell you they are from the Panhandle, you will know exactly how they are going to think and how they will behave.

Hereford was actually considered one of the biggest of the small towns. We felt special (except when compared to Amarillo). And like all the towns, football was king as well as country dancing and Coors Light. We all knew people from the other towns and we all traveled to various parties and festivals.

There was the XIT Rodeo in Dalhart, German Fest in Nazareth, and the Bob Wills Day Festival in Turkey. Also, there were tons of barn dances. Yes, you read that right. There were so many farmers that barns were plentiful and a great place for a dance. Lots of high school kids worked as disc jockeys on the weekends and if there was a barn dance in a 60 mile radius, everyone went.

When we moved to Hereford, it was midway through my 2nd grade year and we remained there through my high school graduation. So, this is where I spent my formative years. Although Hereford only had a population of 15,000, it was full of highly intelligent, well-educated families. It was a major cattle and farming town. Back in those days there was a lot of money to be made in cattle and farming.

Although Hereford was small and located on flat land with few trees, it was actually a pretty little town. There were lots of public parks, a cute downtown, a small mall, a movie theatre and just about anything you might need. At age 8 or 9, we were allowed to roam freely; nothing was really off limits. I remember riding my bike all over town or walking with friends. We congregated at the TG&Y and bought candy from Allsup's. We spent hours running around the little mall or at the skating rink. We had our parents drop us off at Pizza Hut or Taco Villa and wouldn't think a thing of trekking back home by ourselves. We would sometimes take the back road and run through the cemetery. Not once did I ever call to check in. Not once.

Hereford was also near to the skiing mountains of New Mexico. We skied so much that there was a random holiday in February just so that everyone could go skiing. Occasionally we might make it up to Colorado, but in just a 4-5 hour drive, you could be skiing at Angel Fire, Red River, Taos, or my favorite, Ruidoso. Everyone I knew went skiing. And we were allowed to go off on our own even then. I learned to ski at 8 years old and I was good. I would go off on my own, ride the chair lifts on my own, hang with my friends and meet my parents back at the ski lodge at 5ish. Many of the churches in Hereford also sponsored ski trips and it seemed that on any given weekend in the winter, you could find someone from Hereford in New Mexico. New Mexico tolerated us Texans, but we really annoyed the people in Colorado. Both New Mexico and Colorado are in the Mountain Time Zone and Texas is in the Central Time Zone. I remember that we would all ask "what time is it OUR time" and the Coloradans would just grimace.

In Hereford we settled in to a nice 3 bedroom, 2 and a half bath home owned by my dad's new church. Because I had changed schools twice already, starting yet another new school midway through second grade didn't faze me at all. Before long, I had a new group of friends, a lot of them remaining friends through high school. At that time, Hereford had 6 elementary schools, 2 junior high schools and 1 high school. We were allowed to do just about anything as long as we were home for dinner.

The grade school years were generally good years. We took family vacations every summer. They were very typical Griswold style - in a station wagon complete with wood paneling. One summer we drove to California and another summer we drove to Colorado. The trips were long and boring, but we saw and experienced amazing things. We couldn't afford to fly or stay in nice hotels, but I appreciated my parents doing what they could to expose us to more of the country. Most summers we went to Port Aransas, Texas and spent a week on the beach. This is where my love of the ocean and the beach started. I looked forward to our trip to Port Aransas every year. It was a 10 hour drive and I couldn't wait to smell the ocean and see the Palm Trees. We stayed in the same condo every year, owned by a friend of my dad's and there was something really nice about having that same summer routine. We went to the beach two or three times each day, played in the waves for hours, built sand castles, and finished the day off in the swimming pool. We would stand on the balcony and feed the seagulls bread and spend the evening beach walk looking for shells and sand dollars. We ate seafood and watched the fishermen at the pier. I loved the beach. I loved everything about it. This particular memory of my childhood is something I will always cherish, and I believe it formed my lifelong love of the beach - how I ended up where I am now.

Back in Hereford we were also members of the Hereford Country Club where we spent many summer days lounging by the pool and taking tennis lessons. I started going to summer sleep away camps the summer after 4th grade, and attended church camp in Ceta Canyon, tennis camp at West Texas State University in Canyon and basketball camp at Wayland Baptist College in Plainview and the most amazing camp ever where I hope to send my daughter, Kanakuk Kamp in Missouri. My summer childhood memories are all good.

As I went through the grades in school, I always had friends and was generally happy. I did well in school. I was smart, but not brilliant, usually got an A in everything and was basically a good kid. Somewhere around 4th grade I started to get a grasp on who I was, where I excelled, and what my deficiencies were. My parents had taken me to a child psychologist in 2nd grade because I seemed so sensitive and I was indeed diagnosed as a highly sensitive person. There really is such a thing. Like most personality types, it has good and bad episodes. I experience great joys, have deep friendships, but also experience deeper lows (although nothing compared to those who suffer from clinical depression). The highly sensitive child/person is simply more sensitive to their emotional and physical environment than others. This can manifest itself in different ways. My relationship with my mother was difficult at this time because she couldn't and still can't understand why things upset me. For some reason during this time (and for many years to come), I was able to form deep friendships with girls, but could hardly mutter a word to a boy. I was also fairly insecure. I was totally secure about my future and that no matter what I did I would be a success, but day to day living became harder. I was keenly aware of the 'In Crowd' and wanted to be part of that group. I cared very much about what other people thought of me and I would become embarrassed easily. I was losing my footing a little bit.

I specifically remember when entering 5th grade how excited I felt to be friends with the most popular girl in the grade. I also had a crush on a boy. One night after gymnastics class, my best friend and I told the boy that we both liked him. I couldn't look at him for the next 2 years while my friend went on to the 5th grade equivalent of dating him. I was very uncomfortable in my own skin which doesn't bode well for Junior High, when the sharks come out. 6th grade was ok, but it was the first winter where I experienced mild depression. Later in life I gravitated to places with milder winters.

Enter Junior High. I went to La Plata Junior High School, grades 7-9. As is the case with so many people, Junior High turned out to be three completely miserable years. I was super skinny, had a big nose, long feet, and braces. This was the 1980s and the era of "nothing comes between me and my Calvins". My friends all pulled on their tightest Jordache or Calvin Klein jeans and I was stuck with the choice of children's clothes or baggy jeans as I couldn't even fill out a junior size 1. I was well aware of how I looked and was not confident enough to overcome my despair. Pretty typical for this age. Although some of the girls seemed to breeze right through. This is when the concept of popular really began. I was not. I did hang with some of the popular girls, I still had friends, but I hated this time in my life.

Although I was painfully shy and insecure with people during Junior High, I still had an adventurous spirit and a lot of drive. I don't know where my drive came from, something I was born with I guess, but I knew my future would be good and I looked forward to the days when Junior High would be behind me. I had no problem fulfilling my dreams, just problems with interpersonal relationships, again Junior High. One of my dreams, highlighting my budding courage and ambition, was to be a cheerleader. I had dreamed of being a cheerleader since my childhood days in Levelland where my beloved babysitter was a cheerleader. I tried out at the end of 7th grade and didn't make it. I was crushed. I tried out again at the end of my 8th grade year and this time I was all alone. Everyone else tried out in a group. I was never afraid of failure always afraid of regret. I knew if I didn't try for cheerleader, I would regret it. Looking back, I don't know what I was thinking. I was never going to win, all of the guys in my class hated me and I would never get their votes. But, when my name was called the girls in the audience cheered and the teachers admired my bravery. I lost. However, as happens sometimes in life when you keep persevering, one of the cheerleaders had to move away and I got to take her place. The last year of Junior High still sucked, but at least I got to be a cheerleader.

There were a few highlights of Junior High although not many. Because there were two Junior Highs in Hereford, there was a great football rivalry. La Plata versus Stanton. It was so much fun. 2 hometown Junior Highs playing in the fancy High School football stadium with everyone in the town coming to watch. There were also rivalries in basketball, both girls and boys. Unfortunately, even with attending basketball camp, I never made the team. Maybe I should feel lucky that all of my defeats in Junior High led to achievements later in life. I kept being told by my parents that failing builds character. But it sure did hurt at the time. I tried out for basketball in 7th and 8th grades and finally gave up in 9th.

The other cool thing about Junior High was the dances. Finally I was old enough to go to a dance. The local churches or community center would have dances almost every weekend. I couldn't wait to go. 7th grade dances were pretty fun, but by 8th and 9th grade, no one really wanted to dance with me and well, it wasn't so much fun anymore. But, in 7th grade, I danced the night away. My favorite tunes were "I Love Rock 'n Roll" by Joan Jett and the Blackhearts and "Centerfold" by the J. Geils Band. The guys all played air guitar and the girls danced like crazy. The slow songs were when you hoped your crush would ask you to dance and then you would make out. Everyone seemed to get their first kiss in 7th grade on the dance floor, but not me. The other thing we learned was how to 2 step. Not the crazy country dancing done today and no line dances for sure. But, good ole fashioned 2 stepping.

Another tradition introduced in Junior High was what we called twirping. This is like Sadie Hawkins day. The girls got to ask out the guys. I couldn't wait. In 7th grade I twirped my biggest crush. Oh did I have a crush on this guy. He said yes and we went to Pizza Hut and off to the dance. Still didn't get my first kiss, but it was fun. Then in 8th and 9th grade, the guys I twirped actually said no. This was my first taste of real depression. And again, very typical in Junior High, but a rough time nonetheless.

During 7-9 grades, I continued to suffer from insecurity. I absolutely could not talk to a boy. And when the boys made me their target for teasing I just withdrew. I think every friend I had at that time had had their first kiss. Everyone was making out on the dance floor. I had not had a boyfriend or a kiss. My friends thought I was a goody two shoes, but I wasn't at all. I wanted to be the fun wild girl, but I was just too insecure to let go. I was excited for High School, I thought it would be a nice change and I couldn't wait to start drinking beer, a rite of passage. It would be my way of showing everyone that I wasn't such a goody goody. At the end of 9th grade, I really think I was the only girl who hadn't kissed a boy. I went to the movie theater with friends (another make out place aside from the dance floor) and a boy from our rival Junior High wanted to kiss me. I felt safe because he wasn't in on the "pick on Nancy" guys from my Junior High. I said sure and got my first kiss. Right there at the Star movie theater at the end of 9th grade. I could go on to High School with at least that part covered. Of course, I never spoke to my first kiss again because I couldn't talk to boys, but it was a success.

The summer before High School turned out to be interesting. A random popular High School guy asked me out on my first date. I went and of course didn't speak the whole evening. I had such a crush because after the last 2 horrible years of Junior High, I couldn't believe I was on this date. But, learning to talk to guys was, well, the first step in a successful relationship. I had a lot to learn.

Luckily enough, my parents recognized in me my adventurous spirit. So, following the 9th grade they sent me to live with friends in Sweden for a month. My grandparents had met this adorable Swedish couple on a cruise. My grandparents, who lived in San Antonio, Texas, were relatively well connected, and as the Swedish couple had expressed an interest in moving to San Antonio to learn the grocery business, my grandfather could help them. The two families became very close. When the Swedes eventually moved back to Sweden, they all remained in touch. The summer after my 8th grade year (think skinny, big nose) we went to San Antonio to visit, and the Swedes were visiting with their family. They had four kids and my age fell in between their youngest two. The brilliant idea was hatched that I would go to Sweden to visit the following summer.

It was one of the best things to ever happen to me. At age 15, I flew alone from Texas to Sweden. I was just coming off of the date where I didn't talk and was glad to get out of town. During this month in Sweden, I grew up. I learned to live in a foreign country and I learned that I could make it. Sweden was amazing! Only the Swedes' younger two kids were still living at home - their daughter, a year younger than me, and their beautiful son who was three years older. In other words, I was 15 and he was 18. This was my first really major crush. Can you imagine sharing a house for a month with a beautiful 18 year old Swede? The month was amazing. We lived in a small town named Lerum about 45 minutes outside of Gothenburg. We were allowed to go to Gothenburg alone whenever we wanted and I almost passed out one night when asked if we were coming home on the 11:00pm bus or 1:00am train??? So much freedom. I felt so grown up and finally, less ugly. Mind you, I never grew to be a great beauty, but at least got to a point where I felt ok about myself. I still couldn't talk to boys, but being in a foreign country really stretched me and greatly helped my self-esteem.

My crush on the Swedish boy must have been evident (although I never spoke to him) because one morning everyone was out except us and he called me into his room and asked my age. I blushed and continued to not speak. I turned around and went back to the kitchen to make pancakes (my assignment every morning). I could've kicked myself. I had only had one kiss by this time. I thought about the boy when I was in the 9th grade at the movie theatre. I so desperately wanted to kiss this beautiful Swedish boy. I daydreamed about having little Swedish blond kids. He was simply the most wonderful boy ever! I guess my blushing and stuttering really clued him in because the next time we were alone, he called me back into his room. He kissed me. Oh my gosh. And then we heard the front door and it was over almost as soon as it had begun. It was only a minute, but that kiss remained with me for years. I still swoon. And I never said a word to him.

When I returned to the States to start High School, I was a new person. I no longer cared so much what others thought. I just wanted to enjoy High School. Plus I had gained weight, which minimized my big nose and I had gotten my braces off. I wasn't beautiful, but I was ok looking and that was good enough. The other amazing thing about High School is when you enter into the 10th grade, the older guys like you. In other words, the senior guys were interested! I no longer felt so hurt by the guys in my class who wouldn't give me the time of day in Junior High.

I entered the 10th grade with tons of friends, and seniors interested in dating us. I also became involved in the band. Yeah, I know all about band geeks and band camp, but in Hereford it was different. Everything and I mean everything revolved around high school football. If you have ever seen the movie, Friday Night Lights, it was us. We even played that team in the movie once (got crushed). So, whether you were in the band, the pep squad, drill team, cheerleader, whatever….it didn't matter. There were no geeks and Friday night was the night to be involved somehow. So, just about every girl I knew was in the band and we had so much fun. Plus, we rocked. We had band practice kind of like football, starting in the summer almost every night, and so we all grew close. Also, Hereford is far from well, just about anywhere, so for the out of town games, we loaded on to buses and drove anywhere from 1-4 hours for the game. Those bus trips will always remain a great memory for me. It was almost like a slumber party, all the girls sitting around chatting (and there were cool guys in the band too!).

So, a couple of weeks into school in my 10th grade year, I was asked out by a senior. We went on our first date and I didn't speak, but little by little I could at least learn to talk about easy shallow topics. Progress! Oh, he was wonderful. We dated on and off that year and in between, I had tons of other dates as did we all. What a 180 from the Junior High days when no one even asked me to dance. I loved it! All of my other friends were dating seniors as well. We all got asked to Homecoming by cool guys, and lived a magical life. Aside from Friday night football games, there were dances afterwards if it was a home game. To this day, those were the most fun dances. This was back in the 1980s and there were no large groups of girls on the dance floor. The guys asked us to dance whether it was fast, slow, or country. You always hoped the guy you had a crush on would ask you just like in Junior High. During the slow dances, everyone made out just like in Junior High. I look back now and it must have seemed so funny to see a room full of people dancing and making out. Also, the guys in Hereford could dance. They could really dance. Country music was a big part of our lives and these guys could dance. I finally had self-esteem, great friends, and could carry on at least a little conversation with a guy.

There was one area where I had trouble, and to this day I am unsure why I became the target. Although I was great friends with many girls, there were some that absolutely hated me. Almost from the first day of high school, they started calling me beak. Yes, I had and still have a beak. Yes, I have a big nose. Yes, I am still bothered by it, but even more afraid of plastic surgery. It was hard. The girls who teased me were actually really cool and I always wanted to be liked by them. Maybe they honed in on my insecurities, who knows. But, having endured endless rejection from the boys in Junior High plus the daily beak comments, I have to look at it as character building. In the following years, I did become friends with some of those girls and they really were cool. I guess every class has to have someone to pick on; it's just part of growing up.

So another interesting thing about Hereford (at least from a female perspective) was the proximity to college guys. There were 2 colleges nearby; West Texas A&M University and Texas Tech University. Most people from Hereford went to these schools and would come home for holidays and summers. We met a bunch of these guys the summer after 10th grade and they were wonderful. I had mastered the art of talking (although I lost it again in college) and these guys were a blast. It was within this group of guys that I found my first love. He was 3 years older, but 4 grades older. He was wonderful. We danced to country music, listened to Bob Wills' music, and drank Scotch. I thought this was it. I would go to college and then marry this man. Life was good. Then it was time to start 11th grade. Hmmmm

Before I get into 11th grade, I want to talk about Hereford in the summers. Living in such a small town required great imaginations. Although there were lots of dances and cruising around to keep us somewhat busy, there were nights of boredom. We drove out into the country all of the time. We parked, we drank, we had lots of fun. We also discovered a vacant farm house and met there often to drink. We even took white shoe polish and traced it around our bodies to make it look like someone had died. White shoe polish played a large role in Hereford, with many windshields falling victim to our graffiti. We also bought spray paint and painted our names on billboards and other things on the roadside. And we stole the Pizza Hut signs announcing specials. We often tied the signs to trees in front of the houses of our friends. We snuck into the Green Acres swimming pool at night. It sounds kind of mischievous now writing this as an adult, but we were all good kids.

I went into 11th grade madly in love. You might say it was puppy love, but it wasn't, it was the real deal. He went back to college and we saw each other about once a month when he would come home to visit. In the meantime, I continued to enjoy High School. This year for football season I was in the drill team. This was a group of about 30 girls who marched around with the band during halftime, but then put on a special dance. It was so much fun. We wore great costumes and continued to travel together for the out of town games. We really formed a bond. Being from Texas in the 1980s, we all had big hair and wore lots of makeup. On the way to the out of town games, we would do each other's hair and makeup. We would talk about boys and it was all good.

The summer before my senior year really solidified my relationship with my college boyfriend. He came home for the summer and we spent almost every evening together. One of the cool things to do in Hereford on weekends and on summer nights was to go cruising in your car and end up in the parking lot of the Handy Hut convenience store. So, I would start the evening with my girlfriends riding around. I would eventually see my boyfriend and then I might hop in the car with him or he would come to my house if curfew was on the horizon. We would sit in the front yard and talk for hours. We really got to know each other and the love grew. What I couldn't see then and didn't realize until years later is that this relationship grew very slowly over a 2 year period. Later in life I would treat relationships like a job, expecting instant results. Yeah, that didn't happen.

My senior year was great. I was friends with the guys in my class (although they were now dating the sophomores of course) and although I had a college boyfriend, I always had a date to various events. To this day I have fond memories of my dates to Homecoming, Key Club Banquet, and Sports Banquet. I was in the drill team again (tried out for cheerleader twice and never made it), and started the fall off great. Now that I was older, I was allowed to drive the 30 minutes to West Texas A&M University to meet up with my boyfriend. I got to see him all of the time. Back then or maybe in this part of the country, no one paid much attention to drinking ages. We could buy alcohol pretty easily; order it in restaurants, or anything else. Everyone drank. Coors light was a favorite….the silver bullet we called it. Our football team made it to the playoffs and our last game, my senior year, was played in the old Texas Stadium, home of the Dallas Cowboys. I danced across the star in the middle of the field with the drill team and felt very lucky.

Not much has been mentioned about my family thus far. We just weren't that close. My mom provided all I needed. She wasn't strict and bought me stylish clothes and had a homemade dinner on the table every night. But we never really talked. I was (and still am) a highly sensitive person and my mom is not. We never connected. She was a good mom, but not the person I would turn to for deep talks or advice. My brother was 4 years younger than me so he was kind of a non-player in my life. My dad continued to be the minister of a local protestant church. It may seem weird to be a preacher's kid, but in small town West Texas, everyone went to church. It was normal. So, all was well at home. Later I would look back at the household and see that it wasn't good to be the Pleasantville family. Expressing emotions just made everyone uncomfortable. It took years to learn to express my emotions and it's still uncomfortable in my family. Later in life when my boyfriend died, I felt uncomfortable sharing my emotions with them.

College. My parents had great experiences in college and wanted me to have the same. They attended the same college, my dad was in a fraternity and my mom was in a sorority. They said it was like the movie Animal House. They got pinned and/or dropped and enjoyed every minute. My mom couldn't imagine life without being in a sorority. I couldn't imagine life in a sorority. It just didn't seem to fit my personality. My whole senior year of high school, my mom was prepping me for sorority life. We went to the meetings; she spent a fortune on my clothes. One of these meetings featured a freshman in college who was telling her stories of being in a sorority. She talked about dressing up as a piece of lettuce because the sorority went to a parade as a salad. Really??? This is what I had to look forward to? I was thinking more along the lines of fake IDs and no curfew.

Before I started college, my parents gave me a wonderful graduation present...summer school at the University of Hawaii. Again, they supported my adventurous personality. I flew to Hawaii for 6 weeks of what proved to be a life changing summer. Again, just like Sweden, I adjusted to a different way of life, loved it and felt good about it. I met people from all over and saw the world through a much bigger lens. Many people were there just for the summer, but there were also permanent students. Most of those people were studying in the field of International Relations or International Business. I knew then that's what I wanted too. Something international (hey, I was only 18 so "something international" was about as specific as I could get when thinking about a major!). I also continued to love the beach culture. I loved how casual everyone was. Both of these things would shape my life in the future.

I landed in Hawaii at the age of 18 in the summer of 1987. I flew there with a group of girls who I barely knew, but at least I wasn't all alone. We bonded quickly. We lived in the dorm which was co-ed. I loved it. It was so easy to meet people, both boys and girls. All of the people in the dorm would go out together and go to the beach together. It was so much fun. I still had my serious boyfriend so my interest in Hawaii was mainly going to the beach. I took one class, world history, which met daily and then I was on the bus to Waikiki. I had a fake ID and six weeks of the most fun I'd ever had. My eyes were opened to a world beyond Texas which I didn't know existed. The laid back beach culture really grabbed my attention. I rarely wore make up and didn't touch my curling iron. I wore casual clothes and felt pretty. I wore shorts to class every day and met tons of people. It was a friendly campus and I even made friends with the guys in the co-ed dorm and could actually talk. I felt so happy and at home. I was in love with the beach culture and thought college life was awesome.

Also, in the summer of 1987 something big was happening in Nicaragua. There was no TV in our dorm room, but the lobby had a TV and we would gather there to watch the 'Iran Contra Affair' unfold, flipping through the channels. I saw enough of the televised hearings that I became intrigued.

What was happening? Arms sales to Iran? Was that country a friend or enemy of the US? Nicaragua? Where's that? What's a Sandinista? My interest in Latin American politics had begun.

Chapter 2: College Years

Back to Texas, back to my boyfriend, and time to start college. I flew in from Hawaii to Lubbock, Texas where my parents and boyfriend were waiting. It was weird. This would be my first experience with counter-culture shock (but not my last). Culture shock happens when you leave home and adjust to a new culture. Usually this is easy for me because it signifies the beginning of an adventure. Counter-culture shock is coming back home from that adventure and feeling like things have changed and you don't fit in anymore. Home doesn't feel like home and you desperately miss the place where you had been. It really is a terrible feeling and one in which you feel completely lost. I didn't suffer from counter-culture shock coming back from Sweden because my friends welcomed me home with open arms and I jumped into high school which I loved. But, coming back from Hawaii was brutal and I wasn't coming "home" really. I spent a couple of nights at home in Hereford before packing up and heading off to college.

Because my experience with college at the University of Hawaii had been so awesome, I was ready to take on the world. Although I missed Hawaii terribly and missed my friends from Hawaii, I was hopeful that I would settle in to life at my new college in Texas quickly. First things first and I wanted to secure my major. I knew that you didn't need to declare a major so early, but I like making decisions and having a plan. I may change that plan a thousand times, but I like to have some type of path to start down. Because I had become interested in all things "international" (I didn't know the difference at that point between studying international business and international relations), when I looked at the list of majors offered at my new college and saw International Relations (as a subset of Political Science) but no International Business it seemed my decision would be easy. So that settled it...I would major in Political Science. Fast decision making and never looking back has been a gift of mine (I have enough bad attributes, but I rock at making decisions) and so onward with my college career.

So, there I was, a freshman in college, ready to take on the world. I had just flown in from a very successful summer at the University of Hawaii. I made an "A" in my one World History class, had made friends, and felt very confident about college life. At this point my expectations were that I would continue to date my boyfriend (who had transferred to a nearby college), join a sorority, and basically just bask in all things beautiful about being in college and being free.

I moved into the dorm and started getting ready for sorority rush. My new roommate was super cool (still one of my best friends) and the girls in the surrounding rooms also seemed quite nice. There were a few girls who seemed fake and many giggled at my heavy West Texas accent. I was getting the sense that this may not be as easy as the University of Hawaii. But on to rush. Every woman in my family on both sides had been in the same sorority at this college. My dad's first cousin was in this sorority which is how he met my aunt who was in this sorority which is how he met my mom who was in this sorority. My dad's first cousin's daughter was also in this sorority and just a few years ahead of me. So, when I say I felt pressure to go through rush and join this sorority, I mean it.

I was still uneasy in this world. It seemed contrived and fake. There was no list of the best sororities, but everyone kind of knew which were good/bad/weird or whatever. There wasn't, however, a sorority full of beach girls with no makeup. This was Texas in the 1980s and hair and makeup were of the utmost importance. I started rush and did all the things I had been prepped to do during my senior year of high school. I smiled, I complimented, but I felt sick. Probably because of my family legacy, I was indeed chosen to join the same sorority that all of my female family members had been in. I remember opening my invitation card and hearing girls screaming (some crying) and me just cringing; I never was a screamer. To this day I am annoyed by big packs of screaming girls. I remember being happy not to disappoint my family, but not feeling all that excited. I really felt like a fish out of water. I missed Hawaii and the friends I had made there. I was suffering culture shock at this new school. It was different from my lovely childhood in Hereford (and certainly different from Hawaii) where people just seemed more down to earth.

So, with invitation card in hand, I pasted on a smile and ran with all of the screaming girls from the main campus to the Greek campus. This was a tradition at this college and I certainly hope that this tradition has died. The guys all lined up on both sides while the girls ran down the middle. It was a complete grope session. I sometimes wonder just exactly how many guys copped a feel of me that day. When I arrived at the sorority house I felt gross and used. I smiled, posed for the new pledge picture and wanted to throw up.

After the horrific experience of rush week, I hoped things would get back to what I thought was college normal. My experience with colleges at this point had been high school visits to West Texas A&M University, Texas Tech University, and of course attending the University of Hawaii. Although these 3 universities were different, what they had in common was a lot of nice people with fake IDs. I couldn't wait to start going out with my new friends, drinking beer, and basically not have to worry about curfew. Unfortunately, I was stuck with 6 months of pledgeship. My life at that time was all about wearing the right clothes, losing a ton of weight to fit in with the skinny (and largely anorexic and bulimic) sorority girls, and not using fake IDs and not drinking because pledges were not supposed to drink. WTF? I was miserable. And I quickly realized that sorority life was not for me. I am all for making friends and being a part of a group, but secret passwords, handshakes, mandatory study hall, a full semester of being a pledge, yuck! Not for me at all.

This particular college had a ton of rich kids. Nothing wrong with being rich. At. All. But, I was from Hereford and I wasn't used to rich kids. They all had nice cars, I had no car, they all had a limitless supply of money and I had no money. And let me tell you, being in a sorority at a school full of rich kids is very expensive. Thank goodness I had worked all through high school and saved a few hundred dollars plus most of my graduation money because I ended up spending every penny of it. My sweet mom sent me $50 a month not realizing how much had changed since she was in college. And getting a job seemed out of the question because I didn't have a car. In my first week of being in a sorority, everyone had purchased a ton of clothes from the greek store with all sorts of sorority insignia, and bought presents for their "big sisters" (the equivalent of a mentor in sorority speak, and I DID get a really cool one). I bought one pair of sorority shorts and some silly trinket for my big sis. I was not going to fit in here.

Well, I thought, maybe the academics would prove to be better than sorority life. So, I showed up for class on the first day with shorts, t-shirt, hair in a ponytail, and no makeup (hadn't I learned my lesson after rush?). That is what I wore to school in Hawaii. But, I quickly realized with girls looking at me snobbishly that I way way out of my league. The girls were all dressed to the nines, looked ready for a magazine photo shoot. Again, I thought, I do not belong here.

At the same time that I was discovering that I hated college and sorority life, I also realized that I didn't want to be with my boyfriend anymore. He was great, but I was so unsure of who I was and so miserable, I just felt I needed to figure things out on my own. I also didn't think I would be ready to get married after college. Being in Hawaii had opened my eyes to a much larger world and there had always been the spirit and fire in my soul to do big things and live in big places. I didn't think I would be ready to settle down, certainly not for a while. Not that I didn't want to marry and have kids one day, but there was so much of life to see and do. I finally made the heartbreaking decision to end my relationship with my amazing boyfriend in my first year of college. It took a while to get over him. I sometimes wondered if I had made a mistake, but I knew, I knew, that I would be filled with regret if I didn't go explore the world. Now I needed to get happy and figure out who I was and how to fit into the world.

I tried really hard to make this college work. I did make some lifelong friends, friends that to this day are special in my life and I am so grateful for these people. I also made it through pledgeship, went to the sorority parties and a handful of fraternity parties, but really hated almost every minute of it. The other problem there was the girl to guy ratio. I can't remember exactly what it was, but something like 4:1. Not that I was looking for a boyfriend, but being shut out of many fraternity parties wasn't fun. Most of the sororities took about 50 new pledges per year and the fraternities maybe 20. That gives you an idea. Also, when a sorority had a party, you invited the guy, took him to dinner, bought him drinks and a party T-shirt. It cost around $100.00 and this was the late 1980s! Luckily I had my savings to spend, but it seemed ridiculous. Plus, not getting asked to many fraternity parties it seemed to not even out at all.

When it was time to start my sophomore year, I had to go back to college early to be on the other side of sorority rush. If I thought going through rush was bad, being on the other side was horrendous. We had pictures of all of the girls on slides. There was no PowerPoint back then and we had an old fashioned slide projector. Every single girl had her own slide and we would go one picture at a time discussing them. Some girls were a shoe in, if they were a legacy (former family members part of the same sorority), if they already had good friends in the sorority, if they had popular reputations from attending some local high school, or if they were really pretty. Many decisions were based on looks alone. We might all laugh at the movie Animal House when they were making fun of the pictures of pledges, but it wasn't far from the truth.

My best friend at the time from high school was one year below me. She came to this same college and went through rush. I naturally stood up and talked about her when her slide came up. I thought she had it made. She was my best friend, she was a legacy, and she was pretty. A perfect trifecta to be in this sorority. I was asked to leave the room so that everyone could take a vote. One of the sorority advisors came out and informed me that she did not make it. So much for sisterhood. I felt completely betrayed and at that moment I knew my time there was limited. What was the point?

I spent the semester trying to decide what to do because I just couldn't see myself at this school for all 4 years. Should I quit my sorority and stay at school or just leave all together? I thought about transferring to either West Texas A&M University or Texas Tech University to at least be in a culture that I knew and where I felt accepted, but I remembered how happy I had been at the University of Hawaii and how I felt totally comfortable in the casual beach culture. Rich or poor, everyone was in beach clothes all of the time. I knew it would be a stretch to go back to Hawaii because of the distance, but I thought that it was not just Hawaii, but any beach culture that I would love. My parents once again supported my adventurous spirit and helped me search for a new school. We came up with Palm Beach Atlantic University (PBAU). Located in West Palm Beach, Florida, we found what I think is one of the coolest campuses ever. I left my first college after 1 ½ years.

Since I was going to be living so far away from home, my parents decided to go ahead and buy me a car. They were not rich (remember, my dad was a minister), but they did fine in Hereford. So, they bought me a car that cost $1000. It was a 1978 Dodge Challenger and perfect for the beach. I would have been laughed off of campus at my old college, but at the beach it was cool. The three of us drove from West Texas to South Florida in the middle of a very cold winter. The three of us were in the front seat with all of my possessions in the back seat and trunk. The heater broke and we covered ourselves with my bed comforter. We looked like total vagabonds, but my parents were rock stars in their support!

PBAU was small, only 1200 students and no Greek system. It was located in downtown West Palm Beach, right on the Intracoastal Waterway across from swanky Palm Beach. It was gorgeous and true to my thoughts about beach culture, it was casual and wonderful. I made friends quickly and aside from the overly religious tone of the school, it was a good place for me. I arrived with a new attitude. I decided to shun the whole drinking hook up culture. I had had enough of that at my former college. We had consumed a lot of alcohol and I was tired of making out with frat guys who didn't remember my name the next day. This time I was determined not to date or drink, but have fun with friends, spend as much time at the beach as possible and continue paving the way towards my career in International Relations (yes, a bit of an idealist!).

I always tend to make big pronouncements and big decisions. I was and am very all or nothing. I do need to work on that, but that explains my decision to stop drinking and dating. Maybe a more balanced person would say cut back on drinking and not make out with a guy unless on a real date. But, me, no I totally quit drinking and quit dating. Looking back, I probably should have dated a little, but I had gotten burned and just didn't think I could handle it. Although I had had such success with my high school boyfriend, I really didn't know how to date anymore.

This is one area in which I wish my mom and I had been closer. She had such an easy time dating and married so young that no advice was passed down. Trust me when I say that I will have multiple talks with my daughter. My parents had been rock stars when encouraging me in my adventures and my future goals, but unfortunately dating was a mystery. College is where many people learn to date and have various relationships. I had become a strong person by pursuing my goals and having successful friendships, but swearing off dating only led me to learn how to date much later in life. When I finally did enter back into the dating world, I did many things wrong. I was so scared of being hurt that I wouldn't open up and so deep relationships couldn't form. I usually dated someone for about 6 weeks before it all fell apart. Also, I never let the men chase me. Because I was so confident and strong in my academic and professional goals, I treated dating the same way. Not that one should play games, but trust me, pursuing a guy generally doesn't work. This dismal failure in the relationship world would haunt me for years.

Back to PBAU. The next couple of years at PBAU were good. I loved the small size and the fact that there was no Greek system. The classes were small and the professors took a genuine interest in the students. I still credit many professors there with shaping the course of my life. They never laughed when I said I wanted to pursue a career in International Relations and helped guide me to make decisions that would help with my future endeavors. The students were also great. Everyone was nice and I never felt looked down upon. I moved into the dorm and immediately started to make friends. I was also broke and got a job at the mall working retail (Hey, I had a car now!). I had spent all of my savings at my former college. I could relax here and regroup. I made a ton of friends and did pretty well academically. I joined the Student Government Association and also did volunteer work in the community. I started out living in the dorm and then moved into my first apartment with 3 other girls. It was awesome!

My first apartment was a 2 bedroom 2 bath and there were four of us. I was a little nervous about leaving dorm life because I loved living amidst a bunch of girls. It was really fun and I didn't know if I would miss out on anything by moving into an apartment. It was midway through my junior year and I was 21. This is actually kind of late to move out as most people did after freshman and certainly sophomore years, but again, I enjoyed it so there was no hurry. I also knew that this would be the last time in my life that I would ever have that experience. The dorms at PBAU were really cool too. There were 4 bedrooms connected to a living room, bathroom, and balcony with ocean view. Yep, you read that right. I had an ocean view at age 20. We would gather in the living room and gossip about boys (I never had any stories of course but I love hearing them!) and generally have a great time.

But, back to apartment living. It turned out to be great. Although I was still sharing a room, it was nice to have a real apartment, a real kitchen, and just generally feel a little more grown up. We lived in an apartment complex right across from the Intracoastal Waterway. Again, beautiful and magical. My roommates were nice although I have lost touch with all but one, I really liked those girls. The school eventually bought the apartment complex and kicked us out. I was furious, but it turned out to be one of the best things that happened. The school found us a house amongst a bunch of rental houses that students lived in. It was like a college block. The houses were old and I am not sure what kind of zoning existed back then, but there was a sidewalk where a modern day alley would be and it was called Mango Promenade. I'll never forget my days living on Mango Promenade. The house was even big enough that I had my very own bedroom. Yes, first semester of senior year was starting off well.

There were now three of us living together as the fourth got married. We had a 2 story house and each had our own room. Up and down the Promenade were old rental houses filled with college students who became our good friends. I still didn't really drink, but I loved a good party and loved to socialize. We all had parties, ran back and forth to each other's houses, and had a ball. We were in to being progressive and alternative (I never really achieved this). The boys surfed by day and we sun bathed and we all danced and partied at night. Looking back, a few drinks wouldn't have hurt! I am still in touch with some of these friends and I thank them all for that semester of college.

I also took up scuba diving while living in Florida. Scuba diving was actually a class offered at PBAU. This was the first of many ocean sports I would take up over my life. Every week we would drive to the dive center and take lessons. First it was classroom lessons then we hit the pool. We learned how to clear our masks, wear a weight belt, manage our air, and swim around the pool with the tank. Next into the dive tank and then finally the ocean. On our first trip out into the ocean, I was to be the first one out of the boat to dive, I was nervous and excited. The dive instructor was also amazingly cute (all men who work in or near the ocean seem to be really handsome!). I jumped in but the current was strong and I started floating away. Cute dive instructor came and got me and we ended up doing our first dive in the Intracoastal Waterway. But, that day I discovered a deeper love of the ocean, one that continues to this day.

Since I was no longer worried about a fake ID and drinking the nights away, I decided to focus on academics and started paving away at my future. I didn't exactly know what a career in International Relations was, but I knew I wanted to be involved in shaping foreign policy when it came to Latin America. I had started down this path at my former college. Much to my surprise and delight I stumbled onto a debate class that spent the entire semester focused on the Iran Contra scandal. This class helped to solidify my desire to work in foreign policy, specifically Latin America. The 80's (I was in college from 1987-1991) was a time rife with conflict in Central America, see the movie Salvador.

Luckily for me, the head of the Political Science department at PBAU had noticed this desire. He encouraged me to study abroad and later to attend graduate school, both of which my parents supported. He said the first thing I needed to do was learn Spanish. I had taken Spanish in high school and college and had fallen flat both times. He said I had to go abroad. So, he arranged for me to spend a summer attending a language institute. I flew off to Mexico the summer after my sophomore year and lived with a Mexican family in Cuernavaca. I attended a wonderful language institute and my love for the Spanish language and the Latin culture continued. Even though my attempts at Spanish in high school and college were pretty much failures, in Mexico I realized that I had a gift for languages. Not that I was smart, but I wasn't afraid to jump in and start talking and that really is the most important part. Going to Mexico was my most nerve wracking moment. My trip to Sweden was to stay with a family that I knew, I went to the University of Hawaii with a small group of people, but I went to Mexico alone. The language institute said that someone would probably be at the airport to get me. Probably??? What??? I threw up on the way to the airport, but by the time that experience was over, I was braver than ever and confident in my abilities to pick up other languages. I couldn't wait for the next adventure.

My professor then steered me towards a semester's 'Study Abroad' program in Costa Rica. I was all for it, but by the time it came around, I had second thoughts. This would be the second semester of my senior year and the first semester had been so incredibly wonderful (think Mango Promenade). Why would I leave now? I had a ton of friends, was enjoying college and I hated the thought of leaving a good situation for the unknown. Plus, I loved living near the ocean and had really gotten into scuba diving. In Costa Rica, I would be living in the capital city, San Jose, which was not even near the ocean.

I went back and forth trying to make the best decision. College had finally gelled for me and I only had one semester left. I loved my friends, I loved living on Mango Promenade, I loved scuba diving. I finally called the assistant to the director of the Study Abroad program and asked her tons of questions about San Jose's proximity to the ocean. She must have thought I was crazy. I didn't ask any hard questions about studying abroad, just asked if I could get to the ocean and how often. She assured me that San Jose was just a few hours from many beaches and that people often went to the beaches on the weekends. I know it sounds silly to be so concerned about the ocean, but it had become a large part of my life and it made me happy. I was not going to leave my friends and my good college life behind unless I could at least still have the ocean. So, with the words ringing in my head that the ocean is accessible, I decided to go to Costa Rica. It was the first time I would make a decision to leave something behind that I loved so much, but not the last. Leaving my comfort zone became commonplace, and I have yet to regret these decisions because they always led to a better life. My professor said that going to Costa Rica would be life changing and he was right.

I arrived in San Jose, Costa Rica in January 1991. As I mentioned before, this was the last semester of my senior year. I wasn't scared, because this was easy after Mexico. This was an established program and all I had to do was show up. I was, however, a bit surly thinking that I may have made a big mistake. I met everyone at the airport in Miami and we all flew down together. I was the only one from my college and there were about 20 students from various colleges around the country. Almost immediately, though, it was clear that this was a super group of people. This group was adventurous, wanted to experience a different culture, wanted to learn a new language, I could go on. Ok, this won't be so bad. I'll hang with these people and get to the ocean as soon as possible.

We arrived at the San Jose International airport and were greeted by the director and some helpers. They drove us to a hostel where we would spend the night and be picked up the next day by our host families. It may seem weird to live with a strange family in a foreign country, but I had recently lived with a family in Mexico and quickly realized that this was the best way to learn a foreign language, plus, you bond with the family, and learn another culture. I loved it in Mexico and had no qualms about it here. I barely remember our first night in the hostel. I remember that a group of us went to eat at Pizza Hut seeking out something familiar in the first night of our 4 month adventure. We would later spend our last night in that same hostel and it was fun looking back over that time. But, back to our first night. After dinner we all went to bed, kind of quiet, not scared but just eager to meet our new families and start the next 4 months. That night the director asked for 3 volunteers to live with families who lived further from San Jose than the rest. I raised my hand immediately, never one to shy away from the next adventure.

Costa Ricans (Ticos) are very warm and friendly people. As the families poured in the next day to pick us up it became evident pretty quickly that this would be a good semester abroad. My family was the last to arrive. My "mom" was only 28 years old and I was 22! I loved it! She asked that I call her Mami because she took her role as host very seriously. Her husband was Papi, her 4 and 5 year old sons were my little brothers and her parents were my abuelos. Period. I came to love this family immensely and continue to love them to this day. They drove me to their home about 45 minutes outside of San Jose to a little "town" called Higuito. It was a modest neighborhood, but the thing with Costa Rica is that the country is so beautiful and the people so proud that even a simple little house was awesome. There were tropical plants and flowers everywhere and beautiful hills and mountains. I had a small bedroom all to myself and that is all I needed. My second night in Costa Rica was good.

My next goal was to get to the beach as soon as possible and go scuba diving in Costa Rica. Although many weekends of our semester abroad program were filled with fabulous field trips, we did have some weekends free. I think I had been in Costa Rica only a couple of weeks before I went to a travel agency in San Jose to arrange a weekend at the beach scuba diving. They arranged for me to fly in a tiny plane from San Jose to Tamarindo which was a tiny beach town in the northwest part of the country. They made hotel and diving arrangements as well. So, with only a couple of weeks in the country under my belt, I managed to take a couple of buses to the airport and hop on a plane headed for the beach. I hate to fly and although small planes may be technically safer, there is no logic in my fear. Just scared to death! We flew at a low altitude over mountains and then dropped down when we neared the ocean. We landed in a field. Yes, we did. It was a dirt landing strip in a field. I started feeling like I was in the middle of the movie "Romancing the Stone". It got better. I was picked up by a nice guy in a truck with chicken wire in the back and we drove across the field and through a river. No joke. I was nervous, scared, and so excited! This was right up my alley in terms of adventure and I wasn't reading about it, but living it. We finally arrived in Tamarindo at a lovely hotel called Pueblo Dorado. Back in those days the hotel rooms didn't have TVs or phones. My host mom was terrified about my trip and I promised to call her. I found one pay phone in the whole town.

I walked around that night exploring the town, but there were only a few hotels and a dirt road. Nothing going on. The next day I went diving with 2 Ticos. They were lovely and held my hair as I threw up over the boat, horribly seasick. Was it wrong to fly before diving or after? I couldn't remember and I hoped I hadn't done it in the wrong order. But, the diving was amazing. The water was so warm that I didn't wear a wetsuit at all. I fell in love with Tamarindo. I walked around again on my second night and it seemed like a ghost down. I went to sleep and woke early to catch a bus back to San Jose. The bus never came, but 2 Americans passing by gave me a ride to Liberia, which was a larger town with a bus terminal. I didn't know these 2 Americans at all, but in the spirit of adventure, getting rides from strangers seemed the norm. I made it back to San Jose and the adventure continued.

The next 4 months were amazing. We were taught the maze of bus routes and were expected to be at the language institute or in our class every day. Most weekends were filled with field trips. The language institute was great. All of us excelled and with so much practice with our host families, we became at least good Spanish conversationalists. Our classes were pretty demanding and stretched all of us, but in a good way. One of our assignments was to go out and interview various community leaders and conduct the interview in Spanish. I was terrified, but did it and with each accomplishment in Spanish my confidence grew. We also all had to take a 2 week assignment out of San Jose and go work and live with different families. I was assigned to an orphanage in the southern part of the country. I lived with a nice couple that didn't have children and worked in the orphanage for 2 weeks. The orphanage was run well and the kids were taken care of, but it broke my heart. I don't know if I am strong enough for that type of work. It takes amazing people to work in an orphanage. I shed a lot of tears over that time. But, I bonded with the kids and realized that I could indeed converse in Spanish and it was much easier with children. I think about those kids from time to time and hope that they all grew up to have nice lives.

During this 4 month period we also traveled to Guatemala and Nicaragua. You might think all of Central America is the same, but the countries are so different. I couldn't believe how much the culture and people changed from one country to the next. Costa Rica is a fairly modern country with no military and well educated people. The Spanish spoken here is grammatically correct and the use of formal words is used more than in some other Spanish speaking countries. Costa Rica did not have a large indigenous population when the Spanish conquered it so there are many people in Costa Rica who are lighter skinned with more European features. Arriving in Guatemala felt like walking into National Geographic magazine. I had never been anywhere like it. Guatemala had a huge indigenous population (think Maya) when the Spanish conquered it and to this day has Maya descendants that still speak a Maya dialect. Whereas Costa Ricans dress similarly to Americans, the Guatemalans wore amazing indigenous clothing that is beautiful with very bright colors, and true to their descendants, the people are shorter and darker. I loved Guatemala. Our last visit was to Nicaragua. This was very special to me because four years earlier I had been watching the Iran Contra hearings on TV. My interest in Latin America was born, and here I was standing in the very country that first caught my attention. The Nicaraguans look, dress and speak differently to people from Guatemala and Costa Rica. They are incredibly friendly. The areas around the lakes are gorgeous as well as some of the beaches. But the sad part about the country is Managua, the capital. It was leveled by an earthquake in the 1970s and never really built back up. It looked like a ghost town, but it wasn't. Visiting these countries in the spring of 1991 was, and still is one of the highlights of my life.

But it was in Costa Rica that my love for the Spanish language and the Latin American culture and politics really solidified. I loved it. I learned to speak, to dance, to appreciate all that their culture had to offer, I learned their history and politics. When the four months were over, I couldn't imagine what was next. Graduate school followed by Washington, DC seemed the obvious choice, but I was more than depressed by the idea of leaving Costa Rica

I also fell in love for the second time. I pretty much didn't date in between my lovely high school boyfriend and the man I met in Costa Rica. The man I met in Costa Rica started out as a typical story. I was on a study abroad program, enamored with the country and swept off my feet by a Latin lover. He was beautiful. He had deep brown eyes and a lovely smile. He was affectionate, sweet, said everything a girl wants to hear. I fell hard. We met at a dance club. I had become very close to a few girls in the study abroad program and we loved to dance. So, off we went every chance we could. Very early into the program we were dancing the night away at a club called Coco Loco. I was asked to dance a slow dance by one of the most handsome men I had ever seen. I still remember the song was "If You Don't Know Me By Now" by Simply Red. At the end of the night he gave me his phone number. My host family had no phone, so it was up to me to make the calls. I called him soon after from a pay phone. I spoke little Spanish and he spoke no English. But, I said "Hola" and he practically yelled "Nancy?" into the phone. Somehow we managed to communicate enough to set up a meeting in a park the following day.

We met in the park and thus began a three month relationship. It was hilarious because of our language barrier, but I credit him with my rapid language improvement. We met frequently during the week after classes and went to local bars, restaurants, dance clubs, and coffee houses. I had a midnight curfew so as long as I made it home by then (and I always did) then all was well. We also took weekend trips to the beach. He was gorgeous and I was smitten.

As I hadn't dated in college like everyone else, I was still highly insecure. I couldn't talk to boys once I developed feelings for them. I didn't want my heart broken. I was so strong in areas of friendship, school, travel, but boys.....nope! So, after about three months into this relationship (close to the end of the study abroad program), my insecurity pushed him away. I was devastated. All of my fears were confirmed. We continued to date off and on for the next two years, never fully committing. This was the start of a cycle that would last twenty years. But, aside from that (or in spite of that, or because of that) I wanted to stay in Costa Rica.

I asked our program director how I could possibly stay in Costa Rica. I was graduating from college so it would be possible to stay if I could find a way to make money. The director said that teaching would be about the only job he could think of for an expat with zero experience in anything! So, I extended my plane ticket by a week, spent the last night with my fellow study abroad students and friends in the same hostel where we had spent our first night, said goodbye the next morning - and hit the pavement. I went to every international school I could in San Jose and applied to be either a junior high or high school history teacher. I had no certification, but there were no requirements in a private school.

I flew back to Florida dejected and graduated from college. I felt so sad to leave Costa Rica. I should have stayed in West Palm Beach, but was depressed and so I packed my bags and moved in with my parents in Louisiana (they had since moved from Texas). There are very few decisions that I have made in my life that I regret, but this was one of them. Even if you have to waitress and work retail and have no money and no time off and have to share an apartment with ten people to make rent DO NOT move home after college. Nothing good comes from it. Nothing super bad happened, my parents were nice enough. I was suffering from counter-culture shock, missing my friends who I had spent every waking moment with for four months, heartbroken over the loss of my Tico boyfriend, and not knowing what my future held.

Chapter 3: My 20s

Sometimes I feel like the luckiest person on earth. After living with my parents in Louisiana for 2 months I got a call from one of the schools I interviewed with in Costa Rica. They wanted to know if I would teach history to 7th and 8th grade! What?!?!?!? Two weeks later I was on a plane to San Jose. I couldn't believe it. I was 22 years old, a recent college graduate, and I was heading back to San Jose, Costa Rica, the one place in the world where I really wanted to be. I had a Bachelor of Arts degree in Political Science and I was about to be a Junior High School history teacher.

I had never even taken one single class in teaching. Being a political science major, I had many classes in history. But could I teach? And Junior High? Weren't these the most difficult years? I drew on past experiences, and with youth on my side, became Miss McCarter. I taught World History to 7th grade and United States History to 8th grade. I was nervous and as I started preparing for the first week, I realized that I would actually need to learn quite a lot of history before I could teach it. I spent my nights preparing for class and my days teaching. I settled in pretty quickly. I loved teaching the kids in Junior High and understood them well. I remembered my tough Junior High years and I was really only 10 years removed from them. I tried to make history fun as well as attending to the emotional well-being of the kids and ended up getting "Favorite Teacher" at the end of my second year. These kids will forever remain special in my heart. As much as I tried to share and give to them, they gave back to me. Years later I flew in to watch this particular 7th grade class graduate from high school. I loved them then and still love them now.

As for living arrangements, I found a cute little rental house in the same neighborhood as my former study abroad program. It was familiar to me and just so happened to be within walking distance of my on and off Tico boyfriend. Costa Rica was considered a Third world country although now it may just be considered a developing country. But, either way, I didn't have many of the conveniences of the United States. It didn't bother me too often, it was adventurous living and that was what I was all about at the time. The house I rented was made of cinder blocks with no hot water heater, no phone, no cable TV, and no furniture or appliances. I slowly bought all that I needed (including a stove and refrigerator) and learned how to use the widow maker shower (there was an electrical device attached to the shower head that heated the water to luke warm as it came out.....and yes, I said electrical!). There was a pay phone down the street that I used twice a month to call my parents collect and other than that I was set.

I didn't have a car and could never have afforded one. The way Costa Rica is set up is that you can live on very little as long as you live like a Tico. The minute you start wanting a North American lifestyle, it will cost you the same as in North America. I had what was considered to be a very good Costa Rica salary. I think it was about $700.00 per month and my rent came to about $115.00. I had plenty to live on Tico style, but a car was out of the question. In order to get to work, I had about a 20 minute walk down a steep hill (which of course I had to walk back up every day) and then catch a public bus which would drop me off about a block away from the school. After that I had to cross a roundabout and I can only imagine how hilarious it must have been to watch a gringo dodging cars every morning.

The school was pre-school through high school; US accredited and filled with really cool teachers. I made friends with quite a few of them. A couple of the other teachers who were young and adventurous like me became very dear friends. We went out in San Jose every other weekend and took the bus to the beach every other weekend. Although I still had a great love for the beach, San Jose was a blast on weekends. Tons of dancing and music and dressing up. San Jose had a great night life. Very soon we discovered the cool bars and clubs, dressed to the nines, went dancing, listened to live music and had a ball.

I also had gotten back in touch with my Tico boyfriend. Why couldn't I have just left that alone? It would have spared me endless heartache. I have no one to blame but myself. I can't remember if I called him to tell him I was back in town, or if I went to his house, of if I found him at his favorite bar. But, I found him and almost all of the weekends that my friends and I were in town we had to go look for him. Yeah, I was that girl. Ugh. There were times that he and I actually dated and he came over to my house for frequent visits. There were also deliriously happy months when his routine would be to come over every day after work, we would talk for hours and I would cook him an American style dinner. But, then he would just disappear for a while. It was an emotional roller coaster and I just couldn't seem to get off. We did have a beautiful friendship at times, I loved his family, but it was tough.

The other weekends that I wasn't dragging my friends through the bars in San Jose we spent at the beach. All of us loved meeting at the bus stop on Fridays to head out to the beach for the weekend. We traveled everywhere by public bus. The bus stop was in a seedy part of town, but we were all street savvy. We knew the bus schedule like the back of our hands and the tricks to getting on the bus even when tickets were sold out. Remember this was a Third World country so things like seats and tickets were all chaotic, not much order. Many times we didn't have seats on the bus, but would stand the whole time or sit on the floor. It never fazed us. We each took a small backpack for the weekend and we were set.

The beach we went to most often was Manuel Antonio. It was a 3 ½ hour bus ride. It was the most beautiful beach I had ever seen. We had the same routine every time we went. We stayed at the least expensive hostel (about $5 a night) ate dinner only to save money (no breakfast or lunch), ate at the same restaurant and ordered the same dish, and went to the beach inside the national park for the day. At nights we danced and drank the night away. It was pure bliss. Those days will forever remain some of my favorite.

We had met many of the locals in Manuel Antonio and they knew when we were coming. A lot of times they would be waiting at the bus stop. We would arrive about 9:30pm, immediately go to one of the cheap hostels, throw our backpacks down and hit our most favorite place, the Mar y Sombra. The music would be blaring and they played a mix of reggae, Latin, and American dance music (I think it was called techno at the time). We alternated between dancing and drinking and we all had a "beach boyfriend". The next morning we would walk past the public beach and say hi to our "boyfriends" and then head into the national park which was full of tourists and very few locals because there was an entrance fee. We had to walk through the park to get to the first of a series of beaches and it was gorgeous. Imagine walking to the beach and passing sloths and monkeys on the way. Total paradise. We would buy freshly squeezed orange juice and then lay out and swim all day.

One time we ventured much further into the national park, past the first beach to a very secluded beach. We thought we were so cool. We laid out all day only to find that the tide had come in and completely blocked our path back out. We tied our towels around our waists and put on our backpacks and had to swim back to the main beach. We were pushed up against rocks and completely bloody by the time we finished, but we were not fazed. We showered, went to the Mar y Sombra for dinner and then 'repeat' from the night before. It was awesome.

Only a few times did our routine differ. One night we heard that there was a great dance club in the nearby town of Quepos. Not ones to miss a party, we decided to go. Of course, still being broke, we hitch hiked there and back. I can't remember if we were coming or going, but in one of the rides, in the back of a truck with chicken wire I met a guy from the United States playing a harmonica. I commented on his harmonica and in a stoned sort of annoyed voice, he told me that it was actually called a harp. Ok.

It is worth mentioning here that we made a handful of trips up to Tamarindo in the northwest part of Costa Rica. It was further away, about a 6 hour bus ride, but we loved it just as much. We always stayed at the Tamarindo Resort (it is closed now but I know the former owner whose son goes to school with my daughter). It appeared in the movie "Endless Summer 2" (I recently met the star of the movie, Wingnut, while surfing). We had the same routine as in Manuel Antonio. From my first visit to Tamarindo in January of 1991 to my last visit in the spring of 1993, it had really started to grow. It wasn't a secret little fishing village anymore. Surfers had discovered it, and although there had been no nightlife to speak of in January of 1991, by the spring of 1993, it was a blast. The Tamarindo Resort (think simple cabins) had a bar and blasted music every night. We really didn't need to venture far to have a great time.

This period of time in Costa Rica, living in San Jose and teaching school, lasted for two years from the age of 22 to 24 years old. Why did I leave? Trust me, I asked myself that question a million times as I was trudging through the snow the following winter in Washington, DC. But, after teaching for two years in Costa Rica, I knew that if I ever wanted a true career in International Relations, I would have to go to graduate school and eventually move to DC, the hub of all things international. If I stayed in Costa Rica, life would be good, but I would always wonder what else I could have done. In order to prepare for graduate school, I needed to take the GRE, research schools and go through the application process. This was a daunting task from Costa Rica back in the early 90s, pre-internet. I knew I needed to spend a year in the United States to get all of that done before I could go back to school. Luckily, one of my dearest friends from my semester abroad in Costa Rica needed a roommate and she lived in Washington, DC.

Before I packed my bags for DC, my good friend / fellow teacher / beach playmate and I decided to embark on a ten day adventure in Guatemala. It didn't matter to us that they had just had a coup which upended the government, or that it was on the State Department list of countries not to visit, we had been living in Central America for two years and we were veterans. So, off we went to Guatemala with no agenda or plans whatsoever. We still didn't have much money, so we would have to travel in Guatemala the same way we did in Costa Rica, by public bus. I had been to Guatemala two years earlier with my study abroad program, but never on my own.

We arrived in hectic, busy Guatemala City and settled on a cheap hotel downtown. The owner called over a travel agent friend to arrange for us to visit Tikal. You can't go to Guatemala and not hike the Mayan ruins, which we did not do on study abroad. Tikal is far away from Guatemala City and all the other places we wanted to visit so we decided to splurge and fly. It was another flight that reminded me of the first time I went to Tamarindo, a tiny plane barely making it over the mountains. I was terrified but we made it. We spent a couple of days hiking around the Mayan ruins in Tikal. I have never been an athletic person although I love sports, and hiking the ruins was difficult. On TV and in books, the temples look like they have nice stairs to climb up. But in reality, they are crumbling with tree roots everywhere, and they are really tall. It was more like hiking a mountain than climbing up ruins. My friend was a great athlete and beat me to the top of each ruin. At one point, all that people at the top could see was my one arm reaching up. I heard a tourist ask my friend if she was going to help me or just leave me hanging there. We laughed about that for days. I made it to the top of that ruin and many others, and that trip remains one of the highlights of my life. Absolutely amazing. We also took a boat ride around a beautiful adjoining lake. Then back to Guatemala City. I must have blacked out because I don't even remember the return plane ride.

By this time I spoke Spanish well, so getting around wasn't too daunting. Once back in Guatemala City we asked about the public bus to Antigua. This is a beautiful old colonial city with amazing Moorish architecture. It really should be on everyone's bucket list. We toured around on our own for a while and then met a nice Guatemalan man who offered to take us to some sites most tourists don't get to see. We agreed and jumped into his car. Looking back it may not have been the wisest decision. I suppose we could have been captured or something worse, but we weren't. He took us to what is still today one of the oddest sites I have ever seen. It was an idol of some sort that all of the people of this small town worshiped. I guess back in the Wild West days of the United States, someone must have made it down here to Guatemala because this idol was a cowboy drinking whiskey. All around this American cowboy were people praying and worshiping and so much incense I could hardly see or breathe. I will never forget that idol.

Next on to Lake Atitlan and the town of Panajachel. We were used to seeing hippies everywhere; Central America is full of hippies. I always wanted to be a hippie, but was just never cool enough to pull it off. Plus I never got into smoking weed. I was a drinker. Panajachel took the word hippie to a whole new level. They were not just hippies, but maybe beatniks, the kind of super cool people you might find in the early 1960s who predated the hippies. They walked around communal style with children in slings. We never could tell who the parents were because they always traveled in a pack. They specifically hung out at one establishment; I hesitate to even call it a bar. It was very dark and smoky and they all sat around playing the bongo drums. I decided that night that yes, I wanted to fit in a little. I was offered pot cookies (not the kind of pot you cook with!) and I readily took them and ate them. For a few hours, I was a beatnik too. And really hungry.

The next day we were back to being just beach girls from Costa Rica. We went into a restaurant and ordered some tortillas. It was all we could afford. We were broke and still only eating one meal a day. In the midst of the hippies and beatniks, we must have looked as if we'd just come out of a Land's End catalogue cover, because in walk two preppy guys that clearly do not belong and they made a beeline to our table looking scared to death. They were businessmen doing business in Guatemala City and were just taking a quick tour of the country. After hearing our story, they invited us to dinner. I think they felt sorry for us being so broke and starving. We ate like crazy for a couple of hours, hardly coming up for air, and before we parted ways, these two preppy businessmen gave us each a Snickers Bar.

Back to Guatemala City to get ready to return to Costa Rica. Wouldn't it be nice if there was just a direct bus from Lake Atitlan to Guatemala City or if we could have afforded a tourist bus? But, no, we would have to take 3 buses. In Costa Rica, the buses are fairly normal. They are similar to the United States, but in Guatemala, remember, it was like walking into a National Geographic magazine. I am not joking when I say that it did indeed look like we were in the middle of a movie. We were sitting next to chickens and goats. The buses were filled with animals, with many people who only spoke a Mayan dialect and no Spanish, and there was no space, no room for even a tiny backpack. Everyone's bags were thrown on top of the bus. Every time we had to get off to wait for the next bus, the driver would crawl on top and throw our backpacks to the ground. And there we would stand, in the middle of nowhere in Guatemala waiting for the next bus. We finally made it to Guatemala City and this time stayed at the absolute cheapest hostel we could find. I wandered into the courtyard to enjoy the last time I would smoke pot on this trip pretending to be a cool hippie chic and sat down next to a guy playing a harmonica. "Nice harmonica" I said, and he turned to me and replied "It's called a harp". Small world.

In the summer of 1993, I moved to Washington, DC to a cool apartment on Capitol Hill with my friend from study abroad and another girl. I loved it! It was so vibrant. I loved being in the city and I loved being able to walk everywhere (no car needed). There were shops, bars, cafes, restaurants and tons of people in their 20s. I still had no money, but also no debt so I was able to start working with what was called a Temp agency. I was not familiar with Temp agencies at all, but it is a great place to start if you are jobless which I was. The idea is that you get assigned to work various administrative jobs to "temporarily" fill in for someone at a company. Many times the companies would use temp agencies if someone was on maternity leave, or they needed someone to fill in while they looked for a permanent hire, or if there was a temporary project and they needed more manpower. I don't know if Temp agencies still exist, but back in those days it was a great way to get your foot in the door with an entry level position. These temp jobs often led to actual employment. It paid hourly, but it was just enough for rent and a little fun. I was deliriously happy and felt so grown up. I got my first temp job at a bank and wore a suit, carried a briefcase, and took the metro downtown. My second job was also at a bank, but this time in the Embassy Division because they needed a Spanish speaker.

My job at Embassy Banking was amazing. I worked with wonderful people, most in their 20s like me and we all became fast friends, spending time together socially as well as at work. I spoke Spanish daily and met diplomats from around the world. I was invited to fabulous parties and lived a very "trendy" lifestyle. My love life was non-existent as I continued down the path of not being able to connect with a guy. Always freezing up when the conversation would turn the least bit deep. But, I made a ton of friends and was happy with work.

This one year of my life in Washington, DC before graduate school really was amazing. I was 24 years old when I moved there from Costa Rica. This is the perfect age to live on Capitol Hill and experience DC. It didn't matter that I was broke because most of the 20 somethings there were. And there were a lot of 20 somethings. Aside from my co-workers, I became friends with a couple of other girls who I remain friends with to this day. It is funny now to look back and know that they attended my 25th birthday party and all we've been through together since then. I would highly recommend moving to DC after college as it is a blast. I quickly learned the metro and bus system. This was a cake walk after Costa Rica.

Life at this time was filled with happy hours. Everyone I knew had a good job at entry level and we were still young enough to be able to work hard and play hard. Almost every day there was a happy hour somewhere and Thursday night was definitely the night to be out. We were always dressed up in our business suits and would hit the bars as soon as 5 o'clock rolled around. Although I was having a blast, I still missed Costa Rica and the Latin culture. DC is a very international city and offers a little of everything. So, aside from making the happy hour rounds, I also hung out on the weekends at super trendy Latin American clubs and continued to dance salsa and meringue. I briefly dated a diplomat from Argentina and loved hanging with his friends and speaking Spanish. It was a fun year and a great year.

The only thing about living in Washington, DC that I didn't like was the winter. Of course it was one of the coldest winters on record and I trudged through the snow to the metro every morning and evening. I knew that DC was where I would end up after graduate school, but that winter I vowed that once I felt that I had accomplished my career goals, I would move somewhere warm. I had spent most of college in West Palm Beach, Florida and the past two and a half years in Costa Rica. I loved the beach, but even more than that I realized that I never wanted to settle anywhere cold. It was too depressing and I didn't want to feel that way every year for six or seven months. Life is too short.

Aside from spending the year at happy hours and Latin clubs, I had also prepared myself for graduate school. I was accepted into the University of San Diego. Going in, I had a ton of confidence and I was excited to get a Master of Arts degree in International Relations and to continue on with my career. As a side note, I actually had people in DC tell me that I was wasting my time and that a Master of Arts degree in International Relations was worthless. So glad I didn't listen. I was happy about being back in warm weather and near a beach. San Diego did not disappoint. To this day it is one of my favorite cities. I started graduate school at the age of 25 with three years of work experience behind me. I felt so grown up because many people came straight from college. I loved my classes and made tons of friends.

I started graduate school in 1994. By this time most of the turmoil in Central America had subsided. Not that some of the countries weren't corrupt, but the Central America of the 1980s was gone. If I continued down the road of specifically studying Latin America like I had initially set out to do, my career prospects would be few. Even Nicaragua by this time had democratic presidential elections. I took various electives and settled on National Security instead as my focus. Because San Diego is such a big Navy town, I became a little familiar with the Navy. I had never really been around the military or knew anyone in the military. But there were a handful of Navy officers in my class and my best friend was dating a Navy officer. I met all of his friends, briefly dated an Ensign and became happy with my national security choice. This time in my life is important because my introduction into the Navy would later play a very large role in my life.

I loved San Diego. Although graduate school was a bit tedious with multiple 30 page papers due and more reading that one can imagine, I liked my classes and loved my new friends. This is where I met some of the most wonderful people in my life. Like me, they wanted to have fun. We formed a group and would go out for drinks after class. All of our classes were at night from 6 to 9 pm to accommodate people who worked. I took out student loans for the whole program as well as working as a graduate fellow for tuition remission. Again, broke, but so used to it. We would go to various bars and restaurants and get the drink specials and the next day talk on the phone every hour so see how far we had gotten on reading or writing. It was hard, but fun. We also stumbled across an out of the way martini bar that would be the setting for many memorable nights.

I would be remiss if I did not mention that towards the end of my two years in San Diego, an amazing group of friends had formed. We were a hybrid of graduate students and Navy officers. My best friend was now married to a Navy officer and his friends and our friends merged. We formed a group and this group ended up traveling far and wide together through the years. We went to each other's birthdays, weddings, showers, you name it and had the time of our lives for years.

Of course, being back in school, I had to inquire about study abroad. I had never been back to Europe since my time in Sweden when I was 15 years old. Because my studies abroad in college had been so successful, I decided to spend the summer after my first year in graduate school in Italy. I attended summer school at the University of Turin where I found graduate level classes in International Marketing and International Finance. They would transfer back to University of San Diego as electives and I was set. The school was only five weeks duration and that left exactly three weeks before and after to travel.

I got a Eurail pass and toured Spain, France, Switzerland, Italy, and Austria. It was amazing. I traveled alone and had no agenda. Traveling in Europe via Eurail in the summer is actually quite easy. There are tons of people from the United

States and other countries backpacking around. I bought a book called "Go Europe" and would pick a city, jump on the train, and then find the most recommended hostel from the book. The great thing about staying in a hostel (not great is the communal living where you sleep with your backpack padlocked to your body) is that you meet people. It is not like a hotel where you are in a room alone. In the hostel, most rooms are like a bunk house and sometimes you aren't even allowed in during the day. So, everyone congregates in the courtyard. It is during these times that everyone shares stories of their adventures. Based on these stories, I would pick the next place I wanted to travel to and sometimes hang out or travel with others for a couple of days. I loved Europe. I headed back to San Diego and finished up grad school. Then back to DC.

I knew Washington, DC was where I needed to be for my career, but leaving San Diego was heartbreaking. I vowed to return one day. I spent the next five years in DC working my way up the ladder. If anyone ever tells you that you cannot achieve your dream, I am here to tell you that they are wrong. It took a while, but I made it. In the meantime, I moved back to Washington, DC in the summer of 1996 without a job and crashed on a friend's sofa. Before long I had a job at an international trade association. Promoting exports was not what I had in mind. It was international in that we were promoting exports, but I didn't care about commodities. I wanted to work in foreign policy. Still, the job paid well and I learned a ton. I was even sent to work in London for six weeks which was amazing. I still felt lucky.

During those years in DC, in my late 20s, I discovered a little place called Dewey Beach, Delaware. It all started in the summer of 1997 when I was 28 years old. My longtime friend (think I crashed on her sofa) wanted to spend a lazy day on the beach. So, in the latter part of the summer, she picked me up early in the morning and we drove a couple of hours to Lewes Beach, Delaware. Lewes is beautiful and calm and the perfect place for us to have a lazy day. We laid on the beach, read the paper, and napped. We then decided to drive down the coast to Ocean City, Maryland to have a yummy seafood dinner. On the way down, we passed through a small town called Dewey Beach. On the right-hand side of the street was a bar with people literally hanging out of it. What was this? We looked at each other and did a quick u-turn. We wanted to be a part of that. Music was blaring, people were dancing and drinking, it was so fun. We ran into one of our friends who looked at us like we were crazy when we said we weren't familiar with Dewey Beach or this random bar called the Starboard.

The following summer in 1998, our friend invited us to Dewey Beach for a real Dewey Beach weekend. We didn't know what we were in for. Our Dewey veteran took us to a beach house that had been rented out by about 20 or so people. We were allowed to crash on the floor and pay a small fee. I heard someone say something about the people renting this particular house were called Dewey delinquents. Yeah, I really didn't know what I was in for. That night changed my life. I met a group of people that would form my social life for many years to come as well as meet lifelong friends. We were nervous about showing up and spending the night in a house where we didn't know anyone. Our Dewey veteran friend had only met one of the guys on a drunken weekend a few weeks prior. What were we doing? We went and got a bunch of beer because who would turn you away if you arrive with alcohol, right?

We arrived at the house and everyone was already drunk. Everyone was nice and it was as I imagined college should have been. Drunk girls and guys everywhere and friendly and talkative. Crashing on the floor may sound awful now that I am old, but back then it was a ball. My two girlfriends and I drank quickly to catch up with everyone else and then we hit the town. We danced and drank and danced and drank. It. Was. So. Much. Fun. It was the land of hookups and complete craziness, spring break for adults and I wanted more. I spent several more summers there, but it all started when I was 29.

The spring of 1998 just prior to my Dewey Beach initiation was one of the best weeks of my life to date. After I finished working in London for my job at the trade association, I flew to Italy to visit my best friend from graduate school. She had married her Navy officer boyfriend and they were stationed in Naples. It just worked out that I was sent to Europe to work while they were there. I flew into Rome and took a train to Naples. I called my friends from a pay phone at the

Naples train station and they directed me to the metro. I came out of the metro to see my best friend and her husband and we were somewhere in Naples, Italy. Let the fun begin.

They drove me through crazy Naples traffic to their house which was more like a villa. It was 2 stories and all of the rooms had balconies. The house key was even one of those big old fashioned keys which was similar to the key in the movie, "Under the Tuscan Sun". We laughed at the key, walked into the house, and my friends pulled out the limoncello from the freezer and said welcome to Italy. I was scheduled to be there for the next week. After the limoncello shot we went to their friend's apartment on a hill overlooking the Naples Bay. It was a total bachelor pad complete with the refrigerator in the living room. So, the four of us (no one had kids yet) spent the next week living as though we were in a movie. Everything we did was accompanied by lots of wine. Their friend was my "boyfriend" for the week. On that first night, my friends left me at his (we will call him Mr. Italy) apartment which was the beginning of our wonderful whirlwind romance.

The next morning, Mr. Italy drove me back to my friends' house. I crawled in bed with my best friend to gossip about the evening as the 2 guys chatted downstairs. Her husband came up to say that Mr. Italy's ears were burning and we should all go and have some fun. Somehow, her husband and Mr. Italy were able to get out of work for the entire week that I was in town. So, after our first wine-fueled night we got on the train for our first outing which was to Pompei. We hired a private guide and had the most amazing day. Halfway through the tour, Mr. Italy grabbed my hand and I knew this would be magical. We all had another crazy night with lots of wine and took off the next day to the Isle of Capri. We were all still in our 20's at the time so hangovers didn't seem to matter.

We boarded the ferry to the Isle of Capri, my best friend, her husband (also a great friend), Mr. Italy and me. Let this sink in a bit. We were going to the Isle of Capri in Italy. One of the most romantic places on earth. We got there and made our way to the famous Blue Grotto. We took a small boat in while someone sang to us and we all kissed. It was a romantic comedy in the making. We then went shopping and noticed we had just enough time to catch the last ferry back to Naples. But, we couldn't find Mr. Italy anywhere. We took the funicular back to the port and boarded the ferry. I was crushed. Mr. Italy would never make it. Then my friend's husband decided I should get off of the ferry. What did I have to lose? Even if I couldn't find Mr. Italy I would at least be spending the night on the Isle of Capri. Not bad. Then in true movie, romantic comedy style, I literally jumped off of the ferry and over water as it was pulling away. I ran back up the funicular to the shopping district frantically looking for Mr. Italy. It was not to be. I ran from store to store and finally, totally dejected with the clothes on my back and credit card in hand, I took the funicular back to port to buy a ferry ticket for the next day and look for a hotel.

As I was standing in line to buy a ferry ticket, Mr. Italy appeared over the horizon. I yelled to him and started running and then he started running with arms outstretched. I am not making this up. We fell into each other's arms. He knew he had missed the last ferry and never imagined that I would have jumped off for him. We had a great night on the Isle of Capri. A few more wine soaked nights later in Naples and it was time for me to fly back to the United States. I had to first take the train to Rome and spend the night. So, to keep on with the spirit of the week, we all went to Rome. We stayed in the Piazza di Fiore in an adorable hotel in a rooftop room which we could only get to by crawling through a window. We had dinner in the Piazza in front of the Pantheon. How could life be so good? I said goodbye the next day with a heavy heart, boarded a plane for DC, and never saw Mr. Italy again.

Back to my career. After 3 years at the international trade association, I started to doubt that my career goals would ever be met. DC is filled with brilliant people and although I had a Master of Arts in International Relations and spoke Spanish, it didn't matter. Everyone else had the same resume if not better (well, a lot better actually). I signed up for continuing education classes at Georgetown in the field of National Security in the hopes of meeting the right people and it turned out to be one of the best decisions of my life. I met amazing people who were also on the same career path. One of the professors took a personal interest in us and our goals and mentored us outside of class. He recommended to me that I take a look at joining the Navy Reserves. What??? He said if

I went into intelligence that the Navy would pay for a top secret clearance and that doors would start to open.

Thank goodness I had just spent two years in San Diego where the Navy was everywhere. It was still somewhat of a foreign concept to me, but with Navy personnel in my classes and my best friend who was now married to a Navy officer (remember Naples?) I thought…..why not? I called a recruiter and about one year later I was sworn in as Petty Officer McCarter or IS3 McCarter. The recruiter would not put my application in to be an officer because of my lack of experience. Other people who worked in the intelligence field as civilians had that advantage over me. I was told that if I spent a couple of years enlisted that I would then have the experience needed to be an officer. So, I did my time enlisted and two and a half years later, I was again sworn in, this time as Ensign McCarter.

Back in the late 90's, the Navy Reserves were much different to how they are now. We were not at war, there was no such thing as 9/11 and basically you just put on your uniform once a month and learned about ships, submarines, and aircraft. It was fun. For two weeks of the year you had to do training, and with the Navy having bases in cool beach towns, I always spent my two weeks in a wonderful place. Over the years I went to Pensacola, New Orleans, Virginia Beach, and San Diego to name a few.

I joined the Navy Reserves in 1997 when I was 28 years old. I really loved it. The way it was designed back then was to accommodate people in their civilian careers. So, there was no real boot camp or months long schooling. Everything was done either one weekend a month or the mandatory two weeks a year. Once I was sworn in, I went into the training program which was once a month for about nine months. It was called Basic Reserve Intelligence Training. It was similar to school. We would have class all day Saturday and Sunday which included lectures, tests, and presentations. It was located at the Office of Naval Intelligence which is in Maryland just outside of Washington, DC. It was a totally new world to me and I loved it! The classes were amazing and really supplemented all that I had learned in graduate school. I couldn't believe my luck.

The decade of my 20's came to a close with me living in Old Town Alexandria, Virginia, in an apartment with no dishwasher, no food disposal, and a refrigerator so old that I had to defrost the freezer on a regular basis. I was still working at the international trade association, had joined the Navy Reserves, and was driving a nerdy 1994 Chevrolet Corsica. Life was pretty good but my career goals had not been achieved, and I wondered if I would ever have to stop collecting quarters for the communal laundry area. How could I be so broke at 29? I trudged on.

Jacqueline, just born, Las Vegas, August 15, 2008

John preparing Jacqueline for a bath,, Las Vegas 2008

Jacqueline's baptism, Las Vegas, 2008

Hawaii 2010

Hiking, Hawaii c.2010

Professional photo shoot, Hawaii, 2010

Hiking, Hawaii

Photo shoot, Hawaii, 2010

Backyard party, Hawaii, c. 2011

Disneyland, 2012

Chapter 4: My 30s and a Baby

I turned 30 on December 1, 1998 and true to my professor's words from the Continuing Education Department at Georgetown University, being an Intelligence Officer in the Navy Reserves and possessing a Top Secret Clearance on my resume did open doors. Before I knew it, I was a Defense Contractor for a large company working on defense assessments for Central/Eastern European countries to gain entry into NATO. At the age of 30, I had arrived! I bought a condo in Alexandria, Virginia, and a used Sebring convertible. I had tons of friends, spent my summers in Dewey Beach, Delaware and my winters in Seven Springs, Pennsylvania (same idea as Dewey just in the winter). I had a ball.

During these days in my early 30's, Washington, DC was amazing. I had met a ton of people through my Dewey Beach connections and we lived it up in DC. Most of us lived in Northern Virginia and every weekend was spent either in Arlington or in DC. We celebrated everyone's birthdays in wild fashion, went to black tie balls, had house parties, and did our fair share of traveling. We went to Las Vegas and Key West for bachelorette parties, Las Vegas and New York City for New Year's Eve celebrations, and New Orleans for Jazz Fest. We were a tight bunch and it was a great social circle to be a part of. I still struck out with long term relationships, but dated a ton, and everything was great. Before long I got my dream job at the United States Department of State.

I started working at the State Department at age 31. I loved it and to this day it was my most favorite job. One year later was 9/11. I worked in a State Department satellite building across the street from the main State Department building. From some of the offices (including my own) there was a magnificent view of the Potomac River. From my office, I looked out over the Kennedy center right into the river. On September 11, 2001, my boss came running into my office to tell me about the planes that had just crashed into the World Trade Center buildings in New York City. A few minutes later he called us into his office. We watched from my boss' corner office window (which had a sweeping view of the Potomac River all the way down to the Pentagon) in horror as the Pentagon burned. Surely this was unrelated to the events in

New York City? But, the smoke was black and we thought maybe a bomb had gone off. No one thought at that moment that a plane had flown into it. We were evacuated and I started the agonizing two and a half hour drive home. The city was chaotic. Traffic wasn't moving and people were actually abandoning their cars. It was also nerve wracking in that no one knew exactly what was going on. Cell phones weren't working and the fighter jets that had been scrambled to fly overhead were breaking the sound barrier which created a sonic boom which sounded like bomb. I learned later that two of my friends had died.

It was such a sad time for everyone, the whole country. My commute to the State Department every day took me right past the Pentagon, past the side where the plane hit. It looked surreal. Fall turned into winter and it was cold and dark. The United States invaded Afghanistan that October and many of my Navy Reserve friends were being called to active duty. I was put on a Coalition Working Group Task Force at the State Department to specifically assist with various aspects of the Afghanistan invasion. I worked shifts from 10 am to 10 pm, holidays and weekends. I had transferred my Navy Reserve duty from the Office of Naval Intelligence in Maryland down to Norfolk Naval Base, to be on a Navy base with ships. One weekend a month I would get off work at 10 pm and drive four hours to Norfolk to complete my reserve weekend. I was sad, tired, and cold. Spring came and then summer and then a set of orders. I was being called up to active duty to serve nine months at Camp Butmir. Where's that?

I had never served even one day on active duty and now I was going to Bosnia and Herzegovina. I was excited for the opportunity, but scared to death. Would they take one look at me, start laughing, and send me home. Would I succeed? Could I pull this off and fit in with the military? Would they think I was a fraud? I was doing well at the State Department, but this was different. It is amazing to me how fast everything happened. One day I was wearing a power suit walking the halls of the State Department and the next, I was wearing camouflage. I flew commercially from Norfolk, Virginia to Rome, Italy. I then boarded a bus to Naples, Italy. It was weird going back to Naples after my romantic comedy week and now as part of the Navy. I spent a week on a Navy base there preparing for my deployment to Bosnia. I wasn't scared for my life. The war had been over for years. I wasn't going to be fighting, but I was scared of the job. Was I up to it?

One thing about the Navy Reserves is that they really know how to prepare a reservist for a deployment. It wasn't handholding, this was the military after all, but they didn't fly me directly to Bosnia, I did have a week in Naples first. I met the team that was in charge of all Navy deployments to the Balkans. The first item on the agenda was to learn to shoot a 9 mm. I had practiced firing the 9 mm a couple of times before in training, but had never qualified and no one was allowed in country without first qualifying. So, off to the gun range. I was nervous. What if I couldn't shoot? Would I be sent back to Norfolk in disgrace? I had to do this. The qualification included shooting with both hands, with one hand (both the right and then the left), on one knee, on the other knee, and magazine changes. I listened intently to everything the instructor told me and with every ounce of concentration I had, so nervous that my knees were shaking, I began to shoot. I ended up doing well enough to get a ribbon put on my uniform! On my last day they issued me several uniforms, a flak jacket, Kevlar, combat boots, and a 9 mm. I had never worn a camouflage uniform before. They handed me boots, rubber band things, pants, t-shirts, shirt, and a hat. They sent me to my room for the last night. I was to show up the next day dressed appropriately, packed, and ready to depart on a Russian made plane across the Adriatic. The last thing they said to me before I went to my room was, "blouse your pant legs like the Marines". What?

One year after 9/11 I was landing at the Sarajevo, Bosnia and Herzegovina International airport in an AN26B unpressurized, jump seat, propeller plane flown by the Lithuanian Air Force dressed in camouflage with a 9 mm on my hip. Yep, I was in the Navy Reserves alright. So much for spending two weeks on the beach in San Diego! I boarded the plane, put in earplugs, and for the next three hours stared at the luggage on the floor in front of me. It was too loud to talk and too cold do anything but sit there and shiver and wonder what on earth I was doing. We landed into what looked like a war zone. That's because it had been a war zone. This was 2002 and Sarajevo had been heavily damaged by the war. The airport had even served as a front line for a while. There were still bunkers and bombed out buildings everywhere. Again, it wasn't dangerous, but I had never stood in a war torn country before. It was incredibly sad.

I stood there at the airport and decided even if I didn't feel the part, I at least had to look the part. I stood tall in my new combat boots, took out a cigarette and lit it. Holy crap. I was the last person to be picked up. Finally a camouflage Humvee turned the corner and a Navy chief asked me if I was LT McCarter. I was. Get in. We drove to the base, Camp Butmir, which was a NATO base near the airport. When we arrived at the gate, I was asked to clear my weapon. What does that mean? I guess my combat boots and cigarette only masked my ignorance for a short time.

The Navy chief helped me get settled. I had my own room in the co-ed barracks but with an all-girl communal bathroom. And next up my work assignment. I was taken to the US National Intelligence Cell (the USNIC). I walked in and no one was expecting me. Somehow my orders never got back to the NIC. They were thrilled to have me, an unexpected worker. Ok, that is good. I was asked about my background and was assigned the job of Political Officer as elections were coming up in Bosnia soon. Coming from the State Department with a Master's Degree in International Relations, I couldn't have been more thrilled. I could do this. And I did.

One thing about deployments that I really like is the bond you form with those around you. We all lived together, worked together, and socialized together. It became like a big family. And the great thing about working on the NATO base is the relaxed rules. We were peacekeepers and the threat was low. The NATO base was filled with military personnel from NATO countries as well as NATO friendly countries. You name the country and they probably had a representative there. Of course, I loved this. I loved being a part of the international community. If I was going to do anything with the military, being a political officer on a NATO base was a great fit. Because Europeans value eating, drinking, and dancing, the base was filled with cafes, bars, and yes, a dance club. We worked 12 hour shifts, but when we weren't working, we could wear civilian clothes and drink and dance the night away. All of the countries celebrated their holidays and independence days and the whole base celebrated. My favorite was Greece. I am not sure what exactly we were celebrating, but there I was dancing the night away holding hands with lines of people, somewhat similar to the dancing in the movie, "My Big Fat Greek Wedding". I also met friends from Holland who are my friends to this day and have visited me in Washington DC, Las Vegas, and Hawaii.

Along with an amazing job and community on base, we were allowed passes to go off base. So, we got to explore Sarajevo. Sarajevo is simply one of the most beautiful cities I have ever been to. I made friends with a group of American girls and we would shop, go to cafes, bars, restaurants, and have a ball. It was idyllic. I was tired, but it was my own fault. I could have just gone to sleep after my shift or spent my one day off napping, but every chance we got, we went into Sarajevo or "out" on base. I took Serbo-Croatian languages classes once a week and although I have long since forgotten how to speak even one word, I learned enough to get around.

The other thing about Sarajevo is that it is cold. Very cold. Sarajevo was home to the 1984 Winter Olympics of course and on our off days we would go skiing. It snowed in November and there was snow on the ground until April. We walked or biked everywhere and so we were always in the elements. The barracks were nice and toasty though, and I would be sweating by the time I was ready for work. It took about 20 minutes to put on all of the layers. On our nights off, we would head to the German bar, drink lots of nice German beer, and then stumble home in the snow often getting into snowball fights and pushing each other down into the snow embankments. I had to serve gate duty one day for about five hours when the base was opened for VIPs. I hopped from one leg to the next, too cold to take off a glove to smoke. I still wanted to look tough, especially guarding the gate with Bosnian police. One day when the sun came out, we all went for coffee at Echos, our favorite base café. We sat outside basking in the sun. Finally it was warm. I went back to work and checked the temperature. It was 42 degrees. The nine months I spent here turned out to be one of the best and most rewarding periods of my life.

Once that time in Bosnia was over, I was scheduled to return to work at the State Department. I was cold and tired and wanted to rest. I was 34. I went to Louisiana first to visit family. The weather was warm and the neighborhoods were beautiful. My brother and sister-in-law had had a baby while I was in Bosnia. I fell madly in love with her. My first niece. I returned to DC in May and it was cold and grey. So I sold my condo (bought before the housing boom, lucky me), made a small fortune and bought an awesome house in Shreveport, Louisiana where my parents, brother, his wife, their daughter and soon to be new son lived. I worked at a non-profit organization (cut my salary in half), hung out with my niece and nephew, made new friends and then the Navy called again. So after two relaxing years in Louisiana, I was off to the Pentagon.

Wow, the Pentagon. Home to 25,000 of the most miserable people in the world. No one ever stops working. You are really not supposed to eat or sleep. Ever. I worked the hardest job I ever had, lost 20lbs, and had no social life. I was terrified of the Pentagon. Initially, when I got my orders, I wasn't too nervous. Hey, I had spent almost a year on active duty two years prior and did a great job. But, this was different. I wasn't going to be a political officer reporting on elections and analyzing the results and how it would affect Europe, no, this time I was an intelligence officer working on the IED issue. IED? Improvised Explosive Device. The learning curve was going to be huge.

The first day I walked up to the Pentagon. I showed my credentials and immediately entered the wrong door. I got in trouble. Then I tried to go through the turn stile and with the rush of unhappy people behind me, I thought this was going to be more dangerous than anything I had done before. You see, in DC there is an order to everything…a ton of unspoken rules. Unless you know this, you get run down and no one cares. For example, in the metro, when going down the escalator, you stand on the right or walk down the left. You don't talk, you don't linger. Well, the doors and turnstile at the Pentagon were the same. I totally screwed it up on the first day, but eventually learned the system and became a pro at entering and leaving. Once passed the death trap of entry, you are welcomed by one of the largest buildings in the area. There is a numbering system that makes sense, but only if you know. The office numbers describe the floor and the wing. Sounds simple, right? Except many wings are closed off and you just have to "know" where to go. I was escorted to my office the first day. From the front door to my office took twelve minutes. I was on my own on day two, got totally lost, but finally found my way. I then became a Pentagon expert. I could find my way anywhere. Then, I went to grab lunch on the same route I took every day and ran straight into drywall. There were about ten of us just standing there staring at drywall. You see, the Pentagon is always under renovation, so on any given day, your route could be blocked. Time to find a new route.

This job completely kicked my butt. I was responsible for reporting on IED's, analyzing their threat, making predictions based on terrorists' activity, weapons cache finds, etc. Before I could report, I had to learn about these IED's. But, with the military, and I am sure many other jobs, you don't have time to learn before you work. I was thrown into the fire. I really sucked at this job for about five months. I got yelled at daily and if not for a couple of amazing mentors, I may have come home in disgrace. But, I finally got it and ended up running the Intelligence cell before I left. I felt a great deal of pride for having done that job. It was hard and I was severely under qualified, but I did it and I did it well. At this point, I was 37. I had achieved my career goals and now I was finally going to return to San Diego. My plan was to move there, get a job, buy a condo, and live there the rest of my life. I had given up on the idea of marriage and kids. I had never had the maternal instinct or felt the race against my biological clock. I was an aunt and loved being an aunt. I did want to find love, but knew that was unlikely. I sold my house in Louisiana, put everything in storage that wouldn't fit into my car and moved to San Diego with no job, determined to live there the rest of my life.

I rented a studio apartment in the famous gas lamp district and transferred to a Navy Reserve unit on Coronado Island. I had a ton of money in savings, no debt, and just enough from my work with the Navy Reserves to live for a while. I beat down every door in that city looking for work. I had an impeccable resume, tons of confidence but came up with nothing. As it turned out, my new Navy Reserve unit was looking for someone to volunteer at an Air Force Base for six months of active duty. It was in Shreveport, Louisiana! My sister-in-law was pregnant with baby #3 and I needed to get back to work so that my resume wouldn't suffer. I could keep applying for jobs in San Diego while working in Shreveport. So, I accepted the active duty job back in Shreveport for six months with plans to return to San Diego. I did not get a single job offer in San Diego. I finally accepted an offer in Las Vegas to work as a civilian at Nellis Air Force Base. It was somewhat close to San Diego so I could keep looking for job there. I saw the job at Nellis as a stop gap until I could return to San Diego.

I moved to Las Vegas in the summer of 2007 at the age of 38. At first I was not happy at all because I wanted to be in San Diego, but very quickly began to enjoy the city. Don't get me wrong, I had been to Las Vegas many many times over the years, but never saw myself living there. The job I got was great and it paid well. The cost of living is so cheap compared to DC and San Diego and I loved living in a 3 bedroom luxury condo. Everyone in the condo complex was single, beautiful, and fun. We gathered every weekend at the pool, drank all day, and went out all night. I never knew anyone's last name. It was a crazy fun time. I never made any real friends because I was busy with my condo friends and work and that was enough. I didn't plan to live there long and so I wasn't concerned with putting down roots.

I met John on my first day of work in August of 2007. He and I were hired to work on a newly awarded contract for the Air Force. He started a week before I did. I was a little nervous on my first day and was glad John was there to show me the ropes. The other members of our team had been working at Nellis Air Force Base for years, John and I were the only new people who had recently moved into town. John met me in the lobby and started showing me around. He seemed nice and he was nice looking. He had just come out of active duty, having served in the Marine Corps for nine years.

We all started working hard on our new project and slowly John and I became friends. We worked side by side eight hours a day, five days a week. He was much younger than me and I thought he was funny and smart. I enjoyed working with him, but that was about it. He seemed like a private guy. We lived very far from each other (Las Vegas is huge) and it didn't seem likely that we would ever hang out outside of work. I kept going out with my condo friends and I didn't know or really care what he did outside of work.

After a few months we began to talk about our weekends. He liked going out in his area of town called Summerlin, and I of course, was always on the strip. He asked me once to text him the next time I was on the strip, and maybe he would meet me. So I did, and we met, and we eventually became friends outside of work too. I was still more interested in hanging with the condo gang, but John was nice and fun to be around. One night I was in the mood for a nice dinner at an upscale restaurant. I wanted to dress up and eat well and drink well. I never went out to eat with the condo gang. We just always went straight to the bars. So I asked John if he would go out to eat with me. It wasn't a date at all. But we ended up having what I call a typical Las Vegas night. Just watch any movie with the word Vegas in the title. We dined at Red Square in the Mandalay Bay Hotel, ate caviar, drank champagne, and then asked the restaurant manager if we could have access to the Foundation Room. The Foundation Room is a private club at the top of the Mandalay Bay with a phenomenal view of the city. If you are dressed well and spend a lot of money at the hotel you can get on the guest list. We'd spent hundreds of dollars on dinner and we were dressed exquisitely. The restaurant manager asked to see our shoes. I guess we passed the nice shoe test because before we knew it, we were on the elevator going up.

The next thing I knew, I was at home with John beside me. Oh no. We worked together. There was no way this could be a good idea. I sent him an email the next day saying that the previous night was a mistake. He sent a nice email back. I was so impressed with our maturity. Wow. I am so mature. We worked on Monday, Tuesday and Wednesday like two mature co-workers before Thanksgiving break on Thursday. Whew! Crisis averted.

I didn't do anything for Thanksgiving. I usually didn't because I would always fly to Louisiana for Christmas and it seemed silly to fly for both holidays. I stayed home and just took it easy. I was really hungry though. I had the typical bachelorette kitchen. In the refrigerator I had a tub of hummus, a Britta water filter, and Lactaid milk. I am not lactose intolerant, but the Lactaid lasts for months. In the pantry, I had bottles of red wine, baked lays, cereal, and a can of artichoke hearts for the occasional artichoke heart dip dinner. I went into the kitchen and without even sitting down, I ate four bowls of cereal in speedy succession, and then ate the artichoke hearts straight out of the can. And why did I have to pee every 30 seconds?

Back to work on Monday. John and I continued to work together with no mention of anything personal. We were just co-workers and friends at work. My lovely friends from Holland (met in Bosnia) decided to come into town for a week and I was busy with them. We went hiking in Red Rock Canyon and then celebrated my 39th birthday at Nobu in the Hard Rock Hotel. They left and a few days later I decided to take a pregnancy test. Of course it would be negative. I mean, I don't even remember my night with John because I was so drunk. It was positive. On my way to work the next day I bought another pregnancy test, but this time it was a different brand. I'll show them. It was positive. On my way home from work, I stopped by a crisis pregnancy center and they administered a pregnancy test. Congratulations! It's positive.

Despite the fact that I'd never had any desire for children of my own, and my inability to have long term relationships meaning I would never have children of my own, I was elated.

I was excited from the minute I found out. I knew I would keep the baby. That was never a question. I was 39, had a great job, good benefits, and was renting a 3 bedroom, 2 bath condo. I was fine.

Fast forward nine months and John became a dad. Someone once told me that a mom becomes a mom when she is pregnant, but a dad becomes a dad when the baby is born. After I delivered the baby, I remember hearing John's voice across the room exclaiming that she was the most beautiful baby that he had ever seen. She totally looked like an alien, of course, but I could hear the love, joy, and sincerity in his voice. I wasn't ready to hold the baby because I had some minor complications that had to be taken care of. I heard the nurse tell John to get out of the way. Quintessential John! I then heard the nurse say that they always give the baby to the mom first. I remember yelling out that it was ok if they gave her to John. So they did. Eventually he handed her to me. Wow. She had such pretty eyes and lips. She was super skinny with long limbs. She had John's legs and derriere. She had John's mouth. Her name was Jacqueline.

John became a great dad. He learned to change diapers, swaddle, and feed. He measured, steamed, rocked and sang. I told him that I had an open door policy and that he could come and see Jacqueline whenever he wanted. We lived about an hour away from each other and so he asked if occasionally he could sleep in the guest room. He went back to work and visited us two or three times a week.

I settled in to the mom routine quite well. I was overjoyed with my new little bundle. I set my phone alarm to go off every 4 hours to feed her. I changed her diaper when needed and otherwise just held her in my arms. I loved it and I loved her. About seven weeks into my ten week maternity leave, John came over and asked if he could move in. I thought it was a little weird and completely unconventional, but he could have the guest room and guest bathroom if he wanted. There was plenty of room. John moved in when Jacqueline was seven weeks old.

We settled into a routine. John quit work and watched Jacqueline during the day and I would take over when I got home from work. I lived for Fridays. I would go buy a bottle of wine and once Jacqueline was down, would drink a glass or two, eat some popcorn and watch a movie. When Jacqueline was awake, I would hold her in my arms almost nonstop and sing to her and play with her. I loved the weekends with this baby.

As much as I enjoyed my job and living in Las Vegas, I really wanted to live near the ocean. So, a few months before Jacqueline's 1st birthday, I told John that I wanted move and that it was my dream to raise Jacqueline by the ocean. By this time I was madly in love with John and we had become a family. We worked together to decide where to move. And lucky me, I got a job offer in Hawaii.

Chapter 5: Hawaii and Death

I told my co-workers of my plan to raise Jacqueline by the ocean and they started calling in favors trying to get me a new job. I was focused on Florida because of the ocean and the low cost of living. I would love to have found a job in California, but John didn't like California and of course, I wanted to make him happy too. I also thought about moving to Shreveport, Louisiana. All of my family was there, I had friends there, I'd enjoyed living there before, the cost of living was low - but there was one problem….Shreveport has no ocean and I wasn't yet prepared to give up that dream.

One day though, I got a call from a recruiter who had seen my resume online. He often had job opportunities pop up in Florida if I wanted to wait, but he had a job in Hawaii that started immediately if I was interested. Hawaii! John and I sat in the living room while Jacqueline was asleep and weighed the pros and cons of living in Hawaii. It would be a new start for us. The job was good with a good salary. We would be near the ocean. Even if we didn't like it, we could stay for a couple of years and look at it as an adventure. Jacqueline was turning one so this was the time to have an adventure; no worries about school. John and I were working together on this decision and on this move. We were finally a family.

Before we left for Hawaii, we had to go through his things and my things and make lots of decisions. We got rid of a few things, and I shipped my car and the rest of our belongings to Hawaii. After everything had gone, we left for Herndon, Virginia, a suburb of Washington, DC for my job training.

We ended up staying at a Residence Inn in Herndon for three months. We had a good time. John took care of Jacqueline during the day while I worked. I got a ride into work so he had the rental car and would take Jacqueline to parks and malls and museums. I loved living so simply. We had shipped our stuff to Hawaii and I loved our simple life in the hotel. We had a 2 bedroom, 2 bath with a small kitchen and we didn't need anything else. I was being paid very well and we went out to eat almost every night and hung out with my friends from the old DC days. We celebrated Jacqueline's 1st birthday and really started coming together as a family. Wow, this might just work after all. Finally the time came to leave and really begin what I thought would be the beginning of a wonderful life together.

We left Virginia for Hawaii filled with optimism. We rented a big house in the suburbs and started our new life. My job was good and my relationship with John was good. We had finally become a couple and now we were a family. He continued to be a stay at home dad and we very much enjoyed all that Hawaii had to offer. I thought life was going to work out. I really did.

The next year was pretty good. I started my new job and liked it well enough. John started graduate school at night. We spent most weekends on the beach or touring a different part of Hawaii.

Jacqueline was now two and a half and I wanted her to enter into preschool when she turned three. I started researching the schools on the whole island. I didn't mind moving. I really didn't like suburbia. I wanted to find a school that started with preschool and went through to elementary so that we wouldn't have to worry about changing once she was in. After doing my research I found two schools in the town of Kailua that started with preschool, one of them went through to 8th grade and the other through to 12th grade. Kailua was a beautiful town and it seemed the perfect setting for the next phase of our lives. So we enrolled Jacqueline in preschool and moved to the other side of the island to what became one of my most favorite towns in the world, Kailua.

The next year was pretty good. I loved Kailua. We had lived one year in the big house in the 'burbs and I quickly realized that that was not the life for me. Kailua is a walking town right on the beach filled with character. We rented a tiny beach cottage, John continued with graduate school, and Jacqueline started preschool. My job was still going well. One night, sitting in Adirondack chairs in our beautiful backyard, John said he didn't know he could be so happy. We had finally arrived.

We lived in our little Kailua cottage together for one and a half years. Kailua property is extremely expensive because it is a charming town right on one of the most beautiful beaches in the world. We lived only two and a half blocks from the beach. We went all the time. Jacqueline had grown to love the beach and the water. She also excelled in preschool. She was charming. The house, or cottage should I say, was tiny. It had only 870 sq feet, but it was all that we could afford. It was a cute house and it came with a big backyard. We sold a bunch of our furniture and we were back to living a more simple life, like the hotel in Virginia. We bought Jacqueline a big swing set and it seemed as though we had it all.

July 31st, 2012. I got a call from a friend who was in school with John. He was worried because John hadn't shown up for class. I knew straight away that John was dead. The next part feels like slow motion. I got off of the phone and laid out clothes because I knew I would eventually get a knock at the door. I crawled into bed with my daughter and fell asleep. I guess the body knows when it needs sleep. Three hours later came the knock, I got up, put on the clothes that I had laid out and opened the door.

"Did you find him?" I asked? "Yes" they answered.

The next several hours were a blur. I didn't cry at all. I went into shock. Shock is very strange. I could feel my whole body going numb from the top down. It's like taking heavy pain killers and feeling them coursing through you. I guess this is triggered so you can cope. There was so much to think about. So many decisions needed to be made. I sat there on the sofa with two friends of John's who'd come to give me the news. I felt like I was in a tunnel. I was desperately sad, but I wanted to get everything done, over, organized so that I could move on. I remember one of the guys saying to me over and over that I was grace under pressure. I guess because I wasn't screaming or crying but just sitting there, silent, numb.

The first order of business was to tell John's family. Because John and I weren't married, I was not the next of kin. The medical examiner needed to talk to the next of kin. I was terrified of John's parents getting this phone call from a stranger. But I couldn't tell them. I decided to tell one of his sisters, she would be able to break it to them gently. The medical examiner gave me until the morning, then he was going to call. I couldn't get hold of John's sister. She was on vacation. I didn't want to call the other sister. She was pregnant – who knows what trouble the upset would cause. Finally I had to call her. She was at work. I wish I'd told her to go home first, but I wasn't thinking clearly and just blurted out that John had died. She started crying. She passed the phone to a friend and I passed my phone to John's friend and they worked out the details to call the medical examiner. Throughout the day, word got around.

I had told John's sister about his death, I had told my out of town friends, and now it was time to start calling my Hawaii friends. Luckily one of John's friends had had the foresight to call our local priest. He came over with holy water and a candle. I also called a psychologist and asked for an opinion about how to break the news to Jacqueline. A handful of friends came over and then reality started to set in.

The first few hours after a death are so strange. It feels like you are not a part of the world. Everything is surreal and it feels like you are just observing what is going on around you, but not really being a part of it. You can hear people talking to you and you can hear yourself responding, but there is a disconnect. I will be forever grateful to the first handful of friends who showed up that morning. They brought food, answered the phone, and sat with me. They all had busy lives and put down everything for me.

Jacqueline was two weeks away from turning four years old. She was young, but old enough to understand at some level that her dad was gone. The psychologist suggested I tell her that her dad had died and he wouldn't be coming back. It would be unfair for me to give her any information that would leave her with hope. I took Jacqueline back into her bedroom and sat her down. How could I tell my beautiful daughter that her dad had died? She adored him. He had been a stay at home dad for three years. They were so close. I told her that he had died and was in heaven and that he wouldn't be coming home. She didn't cry, she just looked at me blankly. She then came into the living room with me and picked up a cross that the priest had left. She held on to that cross all day. She took the cross into her room and it sat on her bedside table all year. She still has it.

I became obsessed with getting all of the administration taken care of. I thought that the sooner I finished the paperwork, the sooner I could start the grieving process, and the sooner I could heal. I called the life insurance companies, the banks, John's work, the airlines, etc. Sometimes when people die, you hear of the spouse immediately calling to collect insurance and you conclude: That's callous, they're only thinking of the money, maybe they played a role in the death. I won't ever think those things again. I called because I wanted to get everything done. No one ever tells you about the administrative tasks dealing with a death. There is so much to do. Little by little I got everything done. I had to hire an attorney to fight for John's last paycheck because we weren't married and Jacqueline was under eighteen. Finally got that done. I had to get a million letters notarized by John's dad to get John's safety deposit box open, and get into his bank accounts. I had to send off a letter to Hawaiian airlines to get a refund for a trip we had planned to take to Australia. I had to go through his stuff and decide what to keep and what to send to his family. The list goes on and I was obsessed. Every day I made a list and checked items off the list. Not one day did I crawl into bed.

John's family was nothing but wonderful. We all worked together and decided to have John cremated in Hawaii and the funeral in Houston where the majority of his family lived. I had the daunting task of picking up his remains at the funeral home to carry them with me on the plane to Houston. I went alone. The funeral home was so nice. They allowed me to sit in a room by myself to say goodbye to John. I held the box of his ashes in my lap and cried, really cried for the first time. I had been so busy and so obsessed. I get that that had been my way of avoiding the reality. But that day in the funeral home, I couldn't escape what had happened. I took the box home and the next day we boarded a plane to Houston. I don't think I will ever recover from taking the ashes with me on the plane. It still makes me sick every time I think about it. I will forever be haunted by this. I got to security and put the box on the conveyor belt. I told the TSA agent what it was and he cleared the belt and let John pass alone. I picked him up on the other side and proceeded to the gate. I got on board the plane and put John under the seat in front of me. How can this be real? This must be a nightmare. This cannot be real. But it was. How was I going to make it? How was I going to keep my composure? How was I going to be a good and strong mom for my daughter? I just held my breath and kept holding it for the next year.

We stayed in Houston for a week before the funeral. We visited John's family everyday as I was hoping that seeing Jacqueline would offer them some type of comfort. I know the pain that I was in, but I still can't fathom what it must be like to lose a child. Jacqueline's 4th birthday was the day before the funeral. John's sister arranged for a big birthday party and invited the whole family. She also had the foresight to invite her friends with kids and even though we didn't know them, we were grateful to have them at the party. Everyone held it together for Jacqueline's birthday. She ate cake, opened presents, and fully enjoyed all of the attention from both sides of the family. I fought back tears as I am sure everyone else did to make it through that party. I have no pictures. It is just a birthday that is best left forgotten I think. The next day was the funeral. It is all a blur. Then after the funeral, Jacqueline and I flew back to Hawaii to start our new life.

How do you do that? I wish I had an answer. I got lots of advice and every piece of advice held some truth. Day by day, just get up, it's a new normal, time helps…..it's all true. Getting up proved to be especially hard. It's like waking up to a nightmare every morning. Not from a nightmare, but to a nightmare. How do you get out of bed and start the day? How do you get your daughter up and ready for pre-kindergarten and get yourself ready for work. How do you work an eight hour day, then leave and take your daughter to ballet, then come home and do homework, and cook dinner, then do bath and bed? How will you have the energy to do this? How? How? Every morning started this way. I can't remember when it ended……slowly……three months, four months, five months? I don't remember, but what I do know is that one day it just wasn't so hard anymore.

So, year one with just me and Jacqueline. She turned four about two weeks after John died. She went into pre-kindergarten at the same school. When we got back to Hawaii, school had already started and Jacqueline had missed a week. I was grateful to be able to take her back there. It would be her second year; she loved it, she was loved by everyone, and I knew she would be good there. It was the Catholic school associated with our church, the perfect family to be a part of. The priest had helped us, the school had helped us. We were a family. Because I worked full time I would have to utilize the before and after school program. When John was alive, we staggered our work hours so that John took her to school and I picked her up. She did go to the after school program then, but only until 3 o'clock. Now, she would be at school from 7 in the morning until 5 in the evening. It seemed like a long day for a four year old in pre-kindergarten, but I didn't have a choice. The ladies that ran the program were like family to us so even though I wasn't doing the vast majority of parenting, I knew she was in good hands.

We also stayed in the same house so we kept a lot the same. No big changes the whole first year. It was really strange. Everything was different. Our house was quiet, routines were different. John had always done the morning routine with Jacqueline and I had the night routine. I didn't know what to do. I always got up early, got ready for work, kissed Jacqueline and John goodbye and headed out the door. John made breakfast for Jacqueline, John got her dressed, John fixed her hair. What did she eat for breakfast?   How do you put a girls' hair in pigtails so perfectly when she is so wiggly? What time do we need to leave the house? Since I was getting to work later, I would have to pick her up later. She was only four and I hated leaving her at school until 5 o'clock every day.

I could tell that Jacqueline was a happy child in her soul, but she missed her dad terribly. She cried herself to sleep every night. I never cried. I don't know if your body is in shock naturally until you are able to handle it, maybe nature's way of taking care of you. Or maybe it was because I was on Prozac now and it numbed my feelings. I don't know. But I lived in a state of shock for a long time. I made it through each day completely numb and still feeling like I wasn't attached to my body. I went to work and did ok at my job, enough to get by but certainly not a rockstar employee. My bosses were wonderful. I managed to get Jacqueline to and from school, to her after school activities, fed and bathed. I managed to do what was required of me, but it was so weird just going through the motions.

I would not have made it though, if it weren't for my friends. They didn't leave me. They didn't just take care of me that first week. They continued taking care of me all year. They never left my side. They all had families, they all were busy, but they still came over. I was so grateful for this amazing group of women. I remember one day a couple of months after John died. I went home and on my doorstep was a container full of frozen chili. I can't look at chili to this day without the visual of it on my doorstep. It was not only very much needed because I was hardly eating, but it was a symbol of the friends I had who were not going to let me fall.

Not only did my Hawaii friends step up, but many friends from around the world. Unfortunately, Hawaii is so far away, that many of my dear friends from the mainland couldn't come visit, but they called and sent cards and were also by my side. Some did make the journey though. About two and a half months after John died, my friend from Seattle came. She flew in and got a room in Waikiki. Jacqueline and I booked a room too for a staycation. We loved Waikiki and very rarely got down there. It was a respite from our life. A fabulous weekend at the historic Moana Surfrider. I hope my friend knows what that weekend meant to us. Another friend from Memphis came for Thanksgiving and we did another staycation in Waikiki complete with Thanksgiving Luau. She also babysat for me as I had to work over the Thanksgiving holiday when Jacqueline was out of school. I will always appreciate her spending Thanksgiving with us. Another friend came from San Francisco. She stayed with us in Kailua; she did my laundry and cooked my meals. I remember just sitting at the kitchen table almost paralyzed while she cooked for me and served me. Each of these visits came at the right time and gave me a lift.

It took months to get into a routine. I woke up every morning confused. Nothing was normal. I burst into tears on school picture day because I couldn't do Jacqueline's hair as well as John had. I took her brush and pigtail holders to school and asked the teacher's aide to help. I just couldn't do it. The teachers, the aides, the administrators all took me under their wings. It was truly a year of leaning on the "village" for help. I never would have made it without the support from her school. Finally two months after John died, I hired a part time nanny.

I was very lucky to have had my high paying job and to be able to reach out and hire help. I know so many people don't have that option. The nanny was great. The first semester of school after John died, Jacqueline was absent nineteen days. The doctor said her immune system was compromised due to stress. She kept getting sick. She had a stomach virus for seven days which left her dehydrated and in the emergency room. She had three ear infections, she had pink eye. Each time, the nanny would come over, take her to the doctor, and nurse her to back to health. But, wasn't that my job? Jacqueline would sob and beg me to stay home and take care of her, but I had no vacation days left and had even been given advanced vacation days when John died. I could not stay home.

I continued to ask myself when would the pain end? When would life be normal? When could I feel attached to my body again? When could I walk down the street not feeling as if I was in tunnel with the world spinning in slow motion around me? I wanted to get through the grieving period. I wanted to live again. I never thought I would. You don't think it will ever end. You forget what it feels like to feel normal. Nothing is normal. During the first six months, my nanny became my friend and a part of our family. She not only came over every time Jacqueline was sick, but she watched Jacqueline during school holidays, her husband put up Christmas lights, they both came over during the holidays to watch football with my family, they helped me with everything. Aside from all of that she came over every single Thursday at 5:00pm. She totally took care of Jacqueline so that I could have one night off. I met with two friends at the same restaurant every week. I don't know what I would have done without her.

This life was starting to work, but I didn't like it. I never saw my four year old and she needed me. She cried herself to sleep every single night. She missed her dad, never saw her mom. I felt I had no choice but to continue on. I had to work, I had to make money. When school started back after the Christmas break, we were finally in a routine. With help from the school and my nanny, we were doing ok. But, I didn't want to do ok. It just didn't feel right.

At the six month point since John's death, things seemed to worsen. How could that be? Wasn't I going through the grieving process like the books said I should? Wasn't I seeing a therapist? Wasn't I on medication? I was supposed to be moving forward. Why did I feel like I was moving backward? I had made it through the holidays. I still don't know the answer to why I felt so bad, but I remember at our Thursday night girls' dinner, I could hardly speak. I left early and went to the parking lot at Kailua Beach Park. I put on the radio and put my seat back all the way. I cried and cried and cried. I felt hopeless. I couldn't go on. I couldn't go through the motions anymore. I couldn't make it until morning. How do you go on? How? I eventually went home, and I did wake up the next morning, I did take Jacqueline to school and I did go to work.

Chapter 6: Costa Rica

Shortly after John died, it occurred to me that I could live anywhere in the world. It looked as though we would be in Kailua forever and that was fine. It was a weird feeling then to realize that I had the whole world at my feet. Should we move or make a life in Kailua? I spent many nights thinking about this. It was all a part of my strategy for trying to speed through the grieving process. My best friend in the whole world lived just north of Los Angeles. I loved California. Should we move close to her? My parents, brother and his family all live in Shreveport, Louisiana. Should we move there so that Jacqueline could have the benefit of growing up with her cousins? Should we stay in Kailua where I have a great job, many friends, and Jacqueline already in a good school? I decided that whatever I did, I could not start a new job because I was barely hanging on as it was and didn't have the energy or strength to start a new job. My parents offered up their house for free so we could move to Louisiana and I wouldn't have to work for a while. But, silly as it sounds, I wanted to grieve by the ocean. Because of my love affair with the ocean I knew I wouldn't make it without it.

Then one night I was browsing the internet, about a month after John had died. I had been thinking about moving to Central America because it was cheap and I would have enough money not to work for a couple of years. I looked at Nicaragua but the beach and good schools were not close enough together. I had hesitated to look at Costa Rica because it was the most expensive of the Central American countries. And, the only good private schools I knew of were in San Jose, which is not on the beach. I did a quick google search of private schools and a school popped up on the beach. I couldn't believe it. I sat there staring at the web page and I knew right at that second that we would move to Costa Rica. Of course there were other things I needed. I wanted to be close to an international airport and this beach community was at least a four hour drive from San Jose. Oh wait, there is a new airport 45 minutes away. Hmmmm. I needed to be able to purchase a cheap condo with cash so that I wouldn't have to worry about rent or mortgage. Oh wait, there were affordable condos for sale. I couldn't believe it. I booked a ticket for Costa Rica the next day. It was still September and the ticket was for March.

It was a pipe dream. These things really don't work. I flew to Costa Rica in March, toured schools, and looked at condos for sale. Everything came together so easily. I always think in life that when things fall into place, you just go with it. I flew back to Hawaii and thought about this big change for a couple of weeks. I was still surviving life and not living. I never saw my daughter. I needed a break. Would I be in Costa Rica forever? How long could I afford not to work? How smart was it to leave a high paying job? Would the risk be worth it? I thought long and hard about why I wanted to do this. Although I desperately wanted a chance to heal, the number one factor for me was to be given a chance to be a mom to my daughter. I didn't want to look back on life with regrets about not spending enough time with her. Even if we stayed in Costa Rica for one year, that would be one year with her, one year that I would never regret.

One month after my trip to Costa Rica, I wired money to an attorney in Costa Rica and bought a condo. We were really going to do this. Was I crazy? I enrolled Jacqueline in the American private school. We were moving to Tamarindo, Costa Rica.

I quit my job and gave myself one month to either sell, give away, or throw away all of our possessions. This turned out to be gut-wrenching. Everything had a memory associated with it. Every time I sold a piece of furniture or took a bag to goodwill I felt like I'd lost a part of my soul. But, we had to start over, we couldn't live in the past. Had we not moved, we would have continued to live in the same house that we had with John. Had we not moved, I would have kept his belongings in our storage shed. This was forcing us to start over. The hardest thing I have ever done. I kept the most sentimental of our possessions and shipped them to Louisiana and then we packed six suitcases and started our journey to Costa Rica.

We arrived in Tamarindo, Costa Rica on July 26th, 2013. It also happened to be John's birthday, but that was just a coincidence. It didn't go unnoticed. I felt sick. Four days after we arrived was the one year anniversary of his death. What have I done? Ok, deep breath, let's start our new life. Moving is always hard, especially when you move somewhere where you know absolutely no one. I was sad and lonely, but I knew that I had made the right decision. Jacqueline and I spent five weeks together before she started school. We hadn't been together for five weeks since I'd been on maternity leave. She blossomed. We swam together, went to the beach together, went out to eat together. I picked her up after school at the bus stop every day at 3. When she was sick I was home with her, when she had a school holiday we traveled together. Even if I was lonely, no one could ever take this time away from us. I kind of knew from the beginning that we wouldn't be in Costa Rica forever, but I had no timeline. We would stay as long as we needed to (or until we ran out of money).

I was still obsessed with healing. I hadn't really faced John's death. I had always been too afraid that if I "lost it" then I couldn't take care of Jacqueline or go to work. Now, I had 8 hours a day to "lose it" and recover in time to pick up

Jacqueline. I started to face John's death. I went running every day. I ran down to the beach and ran up and down and up and down. Sometimes I cried so hard I would have to stop and try to find a hiding place so that no one could see me or hear me. I cried and cried and cried. It is probably good that I didn't really have many friends in the beginning so I was forced to be alone. I couldn't heal unless I faced the pain head on. Slowly I started meeting people. It was hard. I missed my Hawaii friends.

Shortly after we arrived in Costa Rica in July, I read that my most favorite band, Motley Crue, was going to be playing in Las Vegas. Motley Crue is so much more to me than my favorite band. I read their books and listened to their music and they were instrumental in my recovery. They provided me with a much needed escape during the dark days. I could read about their crazy antics and forget about my life for a time each night. I could put on my ipod and run mindlessly to their music. I had already seen them in concert twice, but didn't want to miss this. I felt that if I flew to Las Vegas to see them it would be a bookend of sorts; seeing them after I had moved to Costa Rica.

I booked plane tickets for Jacqueline and myself, and my ever supportive mom booked a plane ticket as well. I would stay at the Hard Rock Hotel and my mom and Jacqueline would stay at Circus Circus. So, after two and a half months in Costa Rica, we were headed to Vegas for a long weekend. It turned out to be an amazing trip. I decided that as I was facing my grief head on, we needed to include Las Vegas. Jacqueline was born there, I met John there, and I needed to revisit some old places. I rented a car and took Jacqueline by the hospital where she was born and by the condo where we first lived with John. I also took her took my old job. We went into the lobby of the building and right to the spot where I met John for the first time. I don't ever need to go back, but I felt a sense of relief telling Jacqueline that right here in this very spot is where I first met your dad.

My mom took Jacqueline for a couple of days and I hung out at the Hard Rock Hotel. The night before the concert I was hanging in the bar when a group of guys came up to me saying that they had an extra ticket for the concert. It was starting in five minutes. I took it and couldn't see where the seat was because I didn't have my glasses (it happens in your 40s). I went in to the concert hall and was taken to about row ten. I couldn't believe it. Little did I know that it would get better. They next day I went into the hotel hair salon to have my hair done for the concert that night, the night I originally had a ticket for. The hairstylist asked my story and I told her all about Motley Crue and how they had been an escape for me. I told her that I had flown in from Costa Rica with my daughter and my mom had flown out to watch her. I was still sitting in the chair with the hairstylist, when a very pretty girl walked by and said, "nice hair". I said "thanks, I'm on my way to see Motley Crue". Little did I know that it was Nikki Sixx's fiancée (now wife). After I got back to my room, the hairstylist called and said that Courtney had heard my story and wanted to introduce me to Nikki! After the concert I got a call from a friend of Courtney's (Afton) to meet her on the concert floor. She led me up to Nikki's dressing room where Nikki, Duff McKagan, Courtney, Afton, and I rubbed shoulders for a while. Oh. My. Gosh.

We flew back to Costa Rica. I was still depressed. The first six months of Costa Rica were hard, but it was a perfect back drop for me to heal. I had to do this. I had to face it in order to get over it. I had loved John and he was the father of my daughter. The hardest part though was Jacqueline. I could handle the tragedy of the death, but how do you console a child when they have lost a parent?

I just spent as much time with Jacqueline as possible. She had seen a therapist in Hawaii so I knew that I was on the right track with her, but it is so sad. She wasn't crying every night now, but she cried often. She missed her dad. She was also becoming afraid that she would lose memories of him. Which she will and has. I was just so thankful that I could be there for her. Lots of hugs, but lots of sadness for me. Watching your daughter sobbing over a lost parent is gut wrenching.

Life continued on in Costa Rica. I met up with friends for coffee, continued running, surfed as much as possible, and hung out with Jacqueline. Then one day I was contacted by House Hunters International. They wanted to make a show using our story. I thought that reliving it again would be healing for me. It was, but it was also brutal. I don't need to relive it anymore, but I'm glad that I did the show. We were told that we had to fly to Hawaii to do the backstory. We had been away only four months. It was too short, the wounds hadn't healed.

We landed in Hawaii in November and would be there a week. We rented a house in the same neighborhood where we once lived. I started crying the minute we landed and cried for a week. I couldn't stop. It was too soon, yet it would be good for me. We went to Jacqueline's old school, our favorite restaurants, saw our lovely friends, and got ready to film. The memories were everywhere. John was everywhere. I couldn't believe he'd died. It had now been one year and four months but it felt like yesterday. When would there be a day when I wasn't sad anymore? Would this ever end? Would the tears stop? Even walking into the grocery store was hard, I was holding back tears as I shopped. I pulled out my Safeway card and remembered signing up for it with John.

We went to film the next day. I told my story about John dying and me wanting to find a way to spend time with Jacqueline and to heal. I told the story about moving to Costa Rica. I cried. We returned to Costa Rica and I spiraled into depression. Was it being in Hawaii and having the scabs pulled of off my fresh wounds? Was it the memory of John that hit me at every turn? Was it missing my wonderful friends? Maybe it was all of it. I crawled into bed for three months. I had never spent time in bed since John had died. You hear people say they were in bed for a week after their loved ones passed, but I never did that. I kept trying to move forward. I kept trying to skip over the painful parts of healing. I wanted it all to go away. That's the thing with grief though. To move forward you have to feel the pain first.

By this time in Costa Rica I had friends, but we hadn't formed a close bond (not like my old friends who had been there for me when John died.) I finally reached out properly to them and I'm so glad I did. There were there for me, I just hadn't realized. They were open to listening to my story, they would not let me fall. They came to my aid and got me out of bed. I emerged a new person and a stronger person by the spring of our first year in Costa Rica. Although Jacqueline and I will always be saddened by John's death, the pain is no longer all consuming. There may be moments on a daily basis when something reminds us of him, but we are good.

As I write this last paragraph, we have been in Costa Rica for 15 months. Jacqueline is in the 1st grade. She speaks Spanish, she surfs, boogie boards, swims, and has tons of friends from around the world. I have more friends than I could have imagined. We meet every Tuesday for a girls' night dinner and I meet up with several of them during the week for beach walks, surfing, lunch, or coffee. I have a friend who is a published author who has encouraged me during the writing of my book. I have friends who call, who check up on me, who care about me. I feel like we have come through the hardest part and have emerged stronger and better. We are happy. What does our future hold? I don't know. Part of me wants to move to Louisiana to be with family. I will always be open to moving back to Hawaii. I will eventually have to make money again. Will we stay in Costa Rica or return to the States? I don't know. What I do know is that for the past 15 months I have been a stay at home mom, I have bonded and connected with my daughter in a way that would never have been possible if I hadn't quit work. I have run, surfed, cried, and written my book. Whatever our future holds will never change the fact that our time in Costa Rica has been the most healing, rewarding experience we could have asked for and we have, indeed, moved forward.

Made in the USA
Middletown, DE
01 June 2015